Jesus is our

# SUPREME COMMANDER

Supreme Commander

Col. Hank Godman
USAF (Ret.)

John 20:21

# SUPREME COMMANDER

by Colonel Henry C. Godman, USAF (Ret.)

with Cliff Dudley

New Leaf Press
Box 1045, Harrison, Ark. 72601

First Edition, 1980
Library of Congress Catalogue Number: 0-89221-076-1
International Standard Book Number: 80-80658

Cover design: Peter Hope

Dedicated to our sons,

Henry Wyatt Godman

and

Louis Kirkwood Godman, III,

and to

all young men and women

who are searching for the answer—

He is Jesus Christ.

# CONTENTS

Preface . . . . . . . . . . . . . . . . . . . . . . . . . . . . . . . . . . .9

Chapter 1     A Lonely Child . . . . . . . . . . . . . . . . . . . . . . . .11

Chapter 2     The Sky Blue Yonder . . . . . . . . . . . . . . . . . . .17

Chapter 3     Medals and the B-17 . . . . . . . . . . . . . . . . . . . .25

Chapter 4     War Begins. . . . . . . . . . . . . . . . . . . . . . . . . .31

Chapter 5     Disaster and Destiny . . . . . . . . . . . . . . . . . . . .37

Chapter 6     The General's Planes . . . . . . . . . . . . . . . . . . . .49

Chapter 7     The Supreme Commander. . . . . . . . . . . . . . . . .59

Chapter 8     Desperate Moments. . . . . . . . . . . . . . . . . . . . .67

Chapter 9     Military Prestige . . . . . . . . . . . . . . . . . . . . . . .73

Chapter 10    Changes. . . . . . . . . . . . . . . . . . . . . . . . . . . .83

Chapter 11    The Ministering Prodigal . . . . . . . . . . . . . . . . .95

Chapter 12    Healing . . . . . . . . . . . . . . . . . . . . . . . . . . .113

# PREFACE

This book is the story and the struggle of a military family who finally found out that Jesus is alive and listening to the anguished cries of His people.

Our hearts go out in love and compassion to parents whose children are leaning toward the world's ways or are already in the world—the scene—where they think it's at and all together.

After offering ourselves to Him, little did we know the height and breadth and the depth of His promises that would be revealed to us. We found that there is no cheap grace—no bargain basement grace for the true disciple.

We found that this life is a continuous spiritual battle to conquer the forces of evil. Worldly ways and methods have no effect and must be discarded. They may win a skirmish, but the battle is the Lord's.

We battled and won. Our son, Henry, is with the Lord.

Henry and Virginia Godman

# A LONELY CHILD

My dad struggled at the controls to get the engine restarted on the "Jenny."

Billy Sentner climbed out on the wing to signal to the crowd to scatter so that they could land the plane on the wide avenue. The crowd didn't understand, and all the more people came out on the street to watch the plane and the wingwalker.

The people at the downtown parade in Columbus, Ohio, were about to witness tragedy and heroism at the same moment. My dad veered from the wide, but crowded, main street and pointed the crippled plane toward a very narrow street. But the plane's fabric was no match for city concrete. The airplane wings were crumpled by the buildings, and my father was killed instantly. Billy Sentner survived.

The year was 1918, and I was four years old.

My earliest recollection of my father was when I was about two years old. I was being taken on a ferry boat across the channel to the U.S. Army Aviation Detachment of the Signal Corps in San Diego to see my father who was a World War I army aviator.

I remember the ocean, the ferry boat, and the sea gulls. And I also remember my father throwing me up in the air and catching me. Other than that, I don't remember too much about my father, except through my grandmother, Mrs. W. D. Adams, telling me how everybody loved him and what a tremendous flyer he was.

My grandmother took charge of me after my father's death because my mother, who had been separated from my father, supposedly couldn't afford to take care of me. My mother was ill from time to time, and she probably was not able to take care of me properly.

So I was raised as a Godman. Living with grandmother was fun, I guess. But I missed my mother and often wondered why I wasn't living with her.

The earliest recollection of any education was in 1922 when my grandmother took me to Miami, Florida, and personally tutored me up to and through the third grade. She took a special interest in me because she was told that I had a mental problem or learning disability.

I remember somebody saying, "Henry can't learn anything and so his grandmother hasn't put him in school." Now, that comment was a terrific blow to my ego later on in my teenage life when I recalled it.

But there was nothing wrong with me. I went to Miami and passed the test for the first, second, and third grades. I learned all my multiplication tables with the help of a ruler slapped (rapped) across my hand.

I believe my grandmother was trying to put all of the love she had for her son on her grandson. I think parents have a regard, perhaps a higher regard than they should have, for the firstborn son.

After being in Miami, I moved to Beverly Hills. It was way out in the country then. Later, my brother Louis and I were sent to Honolulu for a year. That was a delightful time. We had our own rowboat, and we went barefoot for a whole year. What a wonderful year that was in our lives. My brother and I really were beginning to have a degree of happiness.

My grandmother had married a man by the name of William Dennet Adams, a former Shakespearean actor who at one time ran the Honolulu Opera House and later a music store in Honolulu. He was quite a man in the musical scene. He was gregarious, very flamboyant, well liked, and just a beautiful person. I respected him very much.

My happiness and joy were soon to end. My grandparents, along with my aunt's two sons, were going to travel around the world. They felt Louis and I were too young to enjoy it; instead, we were sent to California to the Montezuma Mountain School for Boys near Los Gatos.

We were only nine and ten so perhaps that was the adult thing to do, but we didn't realize it and felt very lonely and unwanted. But we did have each other. We were not in contact with any member of the family at all for over two years except by letters from around the world. My brother and I were close, and we never fought. I was only eighteen months older than Louis, but I seemed to grow a lot faster than he did.

I had the reputation of being a real good fist fighter at the time, and there were a lot of fights. Usually the kids would gather around and ask me to fight somebody. After awhile we entered into the things of the school and studied hard, and that helped us to forget about our personal problems.

One of the comforts of our lives in that particular school was the housemother. She was a gray-haired lady, very kind and very motherly. She'd tuck us in bed at night and would read stories to us out of *Boys' Life.* I remember one story that she read was the "Water Babies." I thought that was just fantastic because it was a story about these little children who were living under water. She was somebody we could hang onto and reach out to for love.

We had church services every Sunday, and I sang in the boys' choir. I don't remember what we sang, but I enjoyed it. I guess that was my first exposure to "religion." After Montezuma my brother and I were sent to a Del Monte Military Academy.

Grandmother was now living at Del Monte, California. We had many conflicts there because of the perversion tendencies of one of the professors. I told my grandmother about this, and I was jerked out of that school real fast. I did get through the eighth grade there and graduated.

We were then sent to the California Military Academy near Palo Alto, California. There we learned how to drill and to march —real well, in fact. Our school entered into some drill competition with other schools and won a second place, but I knew we were better because we carried real rifles, and the first place team, only wooden dummies.

When I went for the first time to a public school, it became very evident that these private schools had not educated me properly. I had a real struggle catching up in my studies, but soon I did.

Our lives seemed to be ones of constant movement and of never being settled. Louis and I were so busy trying to survive in an isolated environment away from the family that we talked very little. I realize now that it is so important to bring your children up in the family and not send them away.

13

We felt that we were neglected but didn't talk seriously about it because boys at that age really can't seem to talk seriously. We wondered, however, where our family was. We felt we weren't a part of a family. Our father was dead, and we were not allowed to live with our mother. We saw her from time to time. Maybe once a year or once every two years we would journey to Los Angeles where she was living and visit her.

The visits were happy times. They did their best to entertain us. We would go to the beach at Venice and swim. It was a good time, but yet it was a boring time. They wanted to visit and talk. We'd say hello, and then we wanted to go out and play.

In 1928 we were moved again to live with my aunt and uncle, Jack Burns, and my aunt's two boys, Louis Gardner and John Gardner. John later became Secretary of Health, Education, and Welfare under President Johnson.

I enrolled at Palo Alto High School and found out that I was still behind a little bit. I had to have some coaching, but for the very first time in my life I found that I was somebody. I discovered they had a swimming team there. I didn't desire to play football or any basketball because I wasn't very good at that, but I knew I could swim. I had never swum in a competitive race, but in the tryouts I beat everybody.

The coach developed my style and gave me a few pointers, and then I started setting records on the Pacific coast in my junior and senior years at Palo Alto High School. Before long I had won a string of gold medals. Of course, the records have been broken many times since then because now little girls are swimming much faster than I used to swim in those days.

One day I went up to Stanford University and beat their star sprinter. They tried to cover it up, but someone leaked it to the press. (Guess who?) Now, for the very first time, I found out that I was admired and looked up to. My aunt took great pride in me, and I started keeping a scrap book.

Even though I was good at swimming, I was reminded almost every day by my aunt that I required tutoring, and I really did. My grades were really not passing in some studies like English. I tried to pretend that it didn't bother me, but it did. I was very sensitive, and it affected me deeper than anyone realized. My brother and I were always being compared with my cousins. My aunt did her very best for us when it came to feeding us well balanced meals. But it seemed to me that we just weren't loved. I became depressed

14

and had deep emotional problems, most of which I kept to myself. I really loved John and Louis Gardner, but there was no way I could ever match John's brilliance.

One day I decided to end it all; there was simply no use of me living. I had bought an Iver Johnson .22 caliber nine shot revolver for target practice. It would be perfect. . . . I wouldn't know what hit me. But before I could carry out my plan, my aunt discovered the gun in my study desk and asked, "Henry, what is this gun doing in your desk?"

"I have it for target practice," was my reply.

"Well," she said, "get rid of it, and do it now."

I obeyed. I always obeyed!

I learned a very important lesson from my stay at my aunt's home: we should never, never compare our children with someone else's.

**My father, Lieutenant Louis Kirkwood Godman.** This photo was taken only months before his death in 1918.

# THE SKY BLUE YONDER

After high school, I went to Menlo Junior College in Menlo Park, California. I didn't have a B plus average in high school, so I could not get into Stanford University without proving myself at the junior college. Again, I was a star swimmer, and I beat practically everybody. I took calculus, physics, and chemistry and did very well. My grade average was high enough that I could enter Stanford as a junior. My objective was to be an aeronautical engineer.

I can remember that every day I wanted to fly an airplane just like my father did. I would build model airplanes, and we'd fly them on weekends. All my time was spent dreaming about airplanes and drawing airplanes in my sleep. I was even thinking in 1931 how to design a jet engine.

Then my whole object in life, after the junior year at Stanford, was to go to West Point and become an army officer. I was determined to follow in my father's footsteps—not because I had to, but because I simply loved the military. Military life was bred into me, I guess—the discipline and the love for the uniform. I went to a prep school in San Francisco called the Drew Preparatory School for West Point. For a whole year I studied such things as ancient history, American history, geometry, and mathematics. They drilled it into me over and over for the West Point examination. They pressured me until I broke and had a nervous breakdown and had to go to bed for days. I took the examination for West Point in the category of a presidential candidate because I was the son of a deceased army officer.

I tied with another boy for the presidential appointment from our area. We had the same exact score, so they went back

17

into our high school records to see which one had the highest grade average, and I lost. After putting in a whole year of my life in the pressure cooker of preparatory school, I was defeated!

I went back to Stanford University as a senior, and shortly after that I left my aunt's house. I just couldn't take the pressure anymore. I wrote my grandmother in Honolulu and asked her if she would give me the allowance she had been sending my aunt. I then moved into a small apartment of my own. I ate all my meals out. In those days you could buy breakfast for twenty-five cents and lunch for thirty-five cents and a big dinner for fifty cents. So the money that I was sent went a long way, especially since my tuition at Stanford was paid.

Well into my senior year someone told me that I could enter into the Army Air Corps flying school if I could qualify by becoming a flying cadet. I wrote my grandmother and told her I was applying for the Army Air Corps flying school at Randolph Field in San Antonio, Texas, and that I really wanted to do this. "Grandma," I continued, "there are former navy pilots here at the Palo Alto airport who can give me twenty-five hours of instruction for $150. They were professional navy fighter pilots and will insure my passing the cadet course at Randolph Field."

She sent me $150 and I began my course. My instructor was Johnny Preston. He was all man and as hard as nails. He was determined that his students would be the very best.

I learned in a Kinner Fleet biplane. We had no intercom, and it was an open cockpit plane. Let me tell you, when I made a mistake, I could hear his voice coming back to me on the slip stream over the roar of the engine. He drilled me like my life depended on it. And I guess it did. After four hours of flying, I took my solo flight. At the end of the course I enlisted in the Army Air Corps. I took my physical exam in San Francisco and was accepted.

I was so elated and the timing was such that I had to leave Stanford just before graduation. I reported to Randolph Field on the first day of July, 1936, as a flying cadet. I was met by the toughest bunch of upperclassmen that I've ever seen in my life. I stood in a brace for three months; I was lower than the commandant's dog. I ran; I never walked. We drilled in the Texas summer heat. It was just heat, heat, heat, drill, drill, drill. I was beginning to wonder if I was in the Air Corps or the infantry. It was 2½ weeks before we began to fly in the primary stage. It wasn't long before I soloed.

Shortly after I arrived at Randolph Field, the West Point of the air, I received a telegram that my mother had died. I was given leave to attend the funeral. I was flown from San Antonio to El Paso, Texas, in one of our fast training planes, a BT-8 by Seversky, and then caught a train into Los Angeles just in time for the funeral. My maternal grandmother and my mother's sisters and brothers were there.

It was a typical Irish (I'm Irish, every bit of me) funeral of mourning, but afterwards, it was, "Well, let's hoist another drink and then get on with life."

My mother's death had no affect on me spiritually or even too emotionally because I had never lived with her. Now I was without a mother or father, but I still had my grandmother who was more like a mother to me, and I had "Auntie Re" who had worked so hard for me.

After two days I went back to flying school on the train. I had missed about a week of flying school, but because I had been so well instructed before, it didn't really hurt me at all.

I really coasted through flying school because of the training that Johnny Preston had given me in Palo Alto. Before I even started flying, the instructor got me aside in the hangar, just stood on the wing of an airplane, and asked, "Why do you want to become a flying cadet and join the Army Air Corps? Do you want to make it a career?"

My reply was, "Because I've wanted to fly all my life. I love airplanes. My father was Louis Kirkwood Godman, sir. Even a field in Ft. Knox, Kentucky, is named after him. And I want to follow in my father's footsteps."

"Well, that's good enough for me," was his reply.

Everything about flying seemed so natural to me. The runways were, for the most part, all grass. The planes, PT-3's, had tail skids. They were "tail draggers." Today, most planes have a tricycle gear with the nose wheel up front and two main wheels behind the center of gravity, so there is a stable platform. But in the old days the center of gravity was behind the main wheel so there was a tendency for the mass of the airplane to veer suddenly and ground loop. That is to say, if you were going down the runway and you didn't keep the plane absolutely straight on the takeoff or on landing, it would make a rapid turn to the right or to the left and wind up in a ball. Pilots soon get the feeling what that airplane wants to do and just stay ahead of it.

My solo flight was pure joy. Nothing bothered me at all. I was waiting for it. When the instructor got out of the airplane, I knew he was going to send me around alone. I had read these stories how a solo flight was scary. Well, it wasn't with me, at all. To me, I had been released and I had been set free. I didn't have anybody in the front to tell me what to do.

There were 155 of us that started in my group at Randolph Field. The instructor had been asking each of us why we wanted to be flying cadets. And you heard every story imaginable. My preliminary stages of instruction were just a breeze, and it wasn't long until I had passed the primary stage and the basic stage. We were flying BT-9's, BT-2's, and even the very, very first AT-6's. At that time they were very tricky airplanes to fly. We also were flying the Seversky BT-8's, built by the Seversky Corporation of Long Island, New York.

As the days progressed, one after another of the young men would be washed out as being unstable or found unsuitable for flying. They either couldn't learn rapidly to fly, or they weren't precise enough. Every now and then one of my classmates would die in a crash, sometimes with an instructor. It was the policy that all of the classmates had to attend the memorial service. It was sad, of course, but it really made very little impression on me, for I would always think that it would be the other guy and that nothing like that would ever happen to me.

The cause of death was usually a spin. It could have even been the fault of the airplane. I think we're all too prone at times when we really can't find the cause of an airplane crash, even today, to attribute it to pilot error. But one time I saw a BT-8 with two people in it spin in from about 5000 feet, and they just simply could not get it out of the spin. It was one of the normal practice tail spins that we all had to learn about.

Several days later I attended the memorial service, and we put the coffins aboard a train. I went to church five times that year because of the death of classmates, and that's the only time that I darkened the door of a church.

Many of the other boys in class did go to church on Sunday because we were set free on weekends. But I just went to town to carouse. You see, I was never in the habit of going to church. I never received any religious training in my youth at all. As a matter of fact, I heard many remarks in my family where they had stated that religion to most people was just an umbrella that they ran under when they got into trouble. And when the rain was over, they would fold up the umbrella and set it aside.

My grandmother did own a Bible, and she did at times attend a Christian Science meeting. It seemed to be the fad in the '20's or the early '30's. It was the thing for the elite to do. Some years after her death I received her Bible, and it was interesting as I thumbed through it to find out how many Scriptures she had underlined, such as the one that says, "If thou shalt confess with thy mouth the Lord Jesus, and shalt believe in thine heart that God hath raised him from the dead, thou shalt be saved."

So she certainly had a knowledge of God. Whether she confessed Him in her heart or not, I do not know, but I hope so.

The little bit of religious training that we had in military school never seemed to penetrate my mind. I can scarcely even remember what happened. Attending the memorial services of my classmates was virtually the only time that I even thought about death. I never knew anything about soul and spirit. And it did not dawn on me that I should ever know God.

I remember one time as a young man in high school in Palo Alto, I thought for awhile that there certainly must be a God. I knew somebody was in charge of this wonderful universe—simply because of how precisely the stars and the moon and the sun rose and set. And there were times when I'd lie on my back in the daytime, and I would try to project my vision up into the sky so far that I could see God. I would take my hand and gently brush away the air and try to see if I could see something.

At night I would look up into the sky, and I would endeavor to search beyond the stars to see if God was up there. I didn't know how to reach Him and certainly nobody had ever told me even how to seek God or how to make a confession, let alone who Jesus was.

In my mind, I'd always heard in school that the United States was a Christian nation, and because I was born and was living in a Christian nation, I guess I thought that that automatically made me a Christian. I didn't have to do anything, and, after all, the government had "In God We Trust" on our money, and so I assumed that that was all there was to it. Actually, I put it out of my mind.

It was strange because the memorial services did not make any impression on me at all. As a matter of fact, I was so calloused at the time that it seemed to cut into our free time. I wasn't resentful, and it indeed was a solemn occasion, but I never thought it would ever be me.

As I already stated, we began with 155 young men, and every now and then we would hear that someone had died, but unless he was in our platoon or in our barracks or very near us, we didn't even remember what he looked like, and the rest of us just went on with our business.

My business, after all, was to graduate—to learn to fly precisely and to be the very best pilot the world would ever know. I was dedicated beyond reason. And shortly before graduation I knew that this would be my life's vocation. I would be a pilot in the U.S. Air Corps my entire life.

At Kelly Field we trained mostly in the P-12's, those beautiful biplane fighters which today are vintage aircraft. You can scarcely even find one now. And, oh, how I prized that airplane. It was a rip-roaring time of flying, diving in open cockpits with goggles and helmets and that gorgeous flying jacket and then comparing stories in the barracks at night.

Now that I was an upperclassman, I didn't have to study so much at night, and graduation was just a few months away. We were sharp pilots. We knew how to fly. As a matter of fact, our instructors had told us the day before graduation that we were the finest flyers at that moment that we'd ever be because we were honed to a razor edge. We all took great pride in that statement.

Those were the days when America took great pride in its servicemen. And when you would walk down the street in that uniform, it immediately commanded respect. How unfortunate it is today that we respect our servicemen so very little.

The washout rate was sixty-six percent, and that even increased my pride because, after all, only one out of three made it. The only person of my family to attend my graduation was my brother Louis and his wife, Jewel. They brought along a girl by the name of Audrey. She was a nineteen-year-old girl that I had dated many times in high school and college.

I was twenty-three when I graduated, absolutely in the prime of life. And after graduation I took a look at her and said, in a daring manner, "Well, Audrey, there certainly isn't any sense of you going back to California. How about marrying me right here?"

She looked at me and said, "Henry, I'll be glad to." And then as though she second-guessed her answer, she said, "Wait a minute; we can't do this. My family is expecting me back." But we tossed reason to the wind and went ahead and were married.

I knew that she was Christian Science and that her mother was a Christian Science practitioner, but I never gave that a second thought. I didn't think of the implications and little did I know how catastrophic the effects of her beliefs would have in our marriage. But you know how love is. It disregards everything and just plunges ahead. She was a very beautiful girl. She was as beautiful as any movie star that you could ever see. But all too soon I realized that beauty wasn't everything.

Soon after our marriage we drove to Langley Field in Hampton Roads, Virginia, where I had been assigned to the Thirty-sixth Pursuit Squadron, Eighth Pursuit Group.

**Flying Cadet Henry C. Godman in December, 1936.** I was the Cadet Battalion Adjutant at Randolph Field, Texas.

23

**1937 at Kelly Field, Texas.** I am standing in front of a P-12 (Boeing) fighter plane.

# MEDALS AND THE B-17

My first several months at Langley were spent really getting the P-30 (PB-2A) to feel a part of me. I was now a second lieutenant, but I really wasn't dry behind the ears yet as far as the Army Air Corps was concerned.

About a year later, I was transferred to the Second Bomb Group where we were equipped with the first thirteen YB-17's that came off the production line in Seattle. They were the latest thing and were worth their weight in gold.

This was the four engine B-17 bomber that became so famous. I was assigned as the chief of armament section in the squadron to take care of the super-secret Norden bombsight, and I was assigned as a copilot-bombardier. Only majors and captains were allowed to touch the pilot controls and sit in the left seat. First Lieutenant LeMay was the operations officer, and we became good friends for many years.

The B-17 was the first modern four engine bomber, and it could fly and fight at 30,000 feet. We were at these higher altitudes even before the oxygen mask was developed. The way we got our life-sustaining oxygen was to get a rubber hose and put a pipe stem in our mouth and just suck on oxygen at these extremely high altitudes. It could have been fatal.

Later, they developed the rubber oxygen masks that were strapped onto our helmets and kept all outside air out, and we breathed in a mixture of oxygen and air through a regulator according to the altitude. It was an automatic mixture device that gave you more oxygen the higher you flew. A lot of times we would fly at higher altitudes and get these tremendous headaches after we landed from lack of oxygen, particularly in the fighter groups.

The B-17 then was really a jewel. It was the most advanced bomber in the world, and we knew it! The Germans couldn't touch it.

I'm afraid all my time with the B-17 took a small toll on my marriage. It was a good marriage, and the days were so anxious and busy—it was a matter of survival.

My pay was $140 a month, plus $70 flying pay. It took some real close management for it to stretch for the entire month. Before I left Langley, we were asked to fly seven B-17's to South America and to Brazil on a good-will mission. We were given, as a result, one of Brazil's highest national medals, the Brazilian Southern Cross. What an honor!

Soon after this I applied for a transfer to Hickam Air Base in Honolulu. I had heard that there was a vacancy there, and I got it. My wife was now expecting our first child. She preceded me on the Matson luxury liner, the *S. S. Lurline*. I, of course, went by army transport ship, and that took me over a month because we went through the Panama Canal.

It was at Hickam that I started flying B-18's. I was soon appointed operations officer for the Twenty-third Bomb Squadron. My squadron commander was Major Saunders; they called him "Blondie" Saunders because of his black beard. He was a baseball player and coached the base baseball team, which took much of his time. So I ran the squadron as the operations officer. In all intents and purposes I had a squadron to run, and what I said was law! I was then promoted to first lieutenant shortly after I arrived. I taught my pilots dead-reckoning navigation and formation flying.

In a short time our first child, Sandra Anne, was born at Schoefield Barracks in April of 1940.

The base was soon crackling with excitement because the B-17's were on their way to replace the B-18's. The people that ferried them across the Pacific turned around and went back to their home stations, and the commander soon realized I was the only one there that could instruct in the B-17's. He came to me and said, "Lieutenant Godman, have you had any time in B-17's?"

"Yes, sir, I've got 365 hours of pilot time," I replied.

"Godman, you're our instructor pilot!" he directed. So when the planes came in, I climbed into the left seat for the very first time and started checking myself out.

Soon I started instructing people in the art of flying, taking off, landing, and navigating the beautiful B-17's. Of course, the instructor has to sit in the right seat, but when you're the one checking out in the plane, you sit in the pilot's seat. What a thrill that was for me, a first lieutenant! Actually, there's no difference except one of prestige. The man in the left seat is the *pilot*, and he's in charge of the airplane just like the captain of an ocean liner —and what he says goes.

By now there was a war in Europe. England, France, and almost all the European countries were under attack, and some were already defeated. There were also the rumors that Japan was getting ready to declare war on the U.S. In fact, they were already fighting in China. They were buying scrap iron by the millions of tons from the U.S. and taking it to Japan to make armaments. We knew that something was in the wind because why would the U.S. bring B-17's to Honolulu all of a sudden?

In September of 1941 Major "Rosie" O'Donnell, who became famous during World War II, was assigned to take the Fourteenth Bomb Squadron from Honolulu to the Philippines. Were we ever excited! I was a first lieutenant and had my own plane and crew.

The feel of war was in our veins, and we wanted some action. This, however, was a test run to see if the B-17 could make it to the Philippines. No U.S. Air Corps bomber or wheeled plane had as yet made a trans-Pacific flight on the route we planned to go. If we made it, we would be the first.

Little did we know that war is hell, death, flaming ships, hot steel, people getting cut in half, dying, and planes spinning as they come down. We never even thought about that, but just the glory of it all. We all knew there was something in the wind. But what? The code word for the Japanese attack on Pearl Harbor was "Divine Wind"; strange, wasn't it?

Just before we left in September, 1941, a Christian Science friend gave me what they call a shirt pocket Bible and a *Science and Health with Key to the Scriptures* by Mary Baker Eddy. I threw that away but kept the Bible. I still have that Bible! I read the four gospels on the long overwater flights from Honolulu to Darwin.

So, full of awe, we left from Honolulu to Midway Island and then to Wake Island. At Wake Island machine guns were loaded, test fired, and readied to ward off an attack should there be one over the Japanese Mandate Islands. We were strung out at five minute intervals, thirteen airplanes in all.

Of course the Japanese knew that we were flying there, but we were never intercepted. There was only very primitive radar, and I guess they couldn't find us.

From Wake Island we flew right into Port Moresby, New Guinea. We passed right over Rabual Harbor on New Britain. The Japanese later took it, and so many of our airplanes were shot down there with so much destruction and death. We never realized as we looked down on that peaceful harbor what was to happen a year later. At Port Moresby we refueled. We then flew from Port Moresby to Darwin, Australia.

The final leg of our journey, from Darwin to Manila, was 2150 miles and seemed terrifically long. All of our bomb bay tanks were filled, so we could still go over 2500 miles with no problem. As we progressed and got within 300 miles of Manila, the weather became very bad. Our weather briefing had not indicated to us that a typhoon was passing Manila. Now that seems incredible to me that we would be allowed to fly into a typhoon.

As we got close to Manila, we were flying about a hundred feet off the water in and out of rain squalls. At times we could see maybe two or three miles ahead of us, and as an island would loom up, we would veer to the left or to the right—talk about frightening!! We were flying under the typhoon!

The closer we got to Manila, the more apprehensive we became. However, we were so busy with the visual approach to Clark Air Base that we really didn't have time to think how frightened we were. We got out all of the maps we could, and we were trying to follow the coastline in making our approach.

We came into Manila Bay exactly like a ship would come in and almost as low! And in the middle of the bay entrance channel was Corregidor! We were right down almost on the water. We came in from the west toward Manila and followed the eastern shoreline of Bataan until we got lined up with Clark Field.

Just to the southeast of Clark Field there was a small pyramid-shaped mountain sticking up one thousand feet or so, and it's called Mt. Ararat. We could see that, so we could get our bearings.

There were no concrete runways in those days, and the runway was just hard-packed sod. The B-17's were somewhat light, at least light enough to land in the sod if it wasn't too muddy.

We had instruments, but at that time there were no good navigational aids. All of us made a safe approach. We were all very young but, oh, how professional we thought we were, and I guess we were. There was very little communication as we made our approaches because we were too busy. I was the second to land, right behind Major O'Donnell; and let me tell you, were there some hair-raising stories that were told about that flight. It was a two flag typhoon. That means just about the worst storm.

We hoisted our drinks and patted each other on the back and were glad that we'd all arrived safely. All of us on that flight received the Distinguished Flying Cross! We all thought that we had arrived.

**The Swoose.** I flew this B-17C from Hickam Field in September of 1941 to the Philippines. I also flew the plane on several combat missions. Later I flew a B-17E, which was equipped with two .50 caliber machine guns in the tail; we shot down two Zeros on the first mission in the E model. (Photo by U.S. Army Signal Corps)

## WAR BEGINS

After the flight across the Pacific we thought we were pretty big men. We were assigned quarters on the base. There were four of us to each house; it was the first time I had lived in a house on stilts.

We were each assigned a houseboy to take care of our uniforms and to do our cooking and things of that sort.

Thinking back to that time, I have to smile as I recall that every time I took off my uniform for an afternoon siesta after lunch, which was the custom there, my uniform would be grabbed up and washed, pressed, and laid back perfectly starched, ready to wear. I told my little Filipino houseboy that he was going to wear my uniform out, and he pretended that he didn't understand me.

And he said, "This, sir, is all I've got to do, and if I don't do it, I'll be fired."

But let me tell you, our uniforms were immaculate.

Gasoline was in somewhat short supply at that time, so we weren't flying and training too much in order to conserve gasoline. But in October and November of 1941 the tension all over the world increased. President Roosevelt and General MacArthur were aware of this tension, and I'm certain that they knew something was going to happen, but they didn't know exactly where.

There was electricity in the air. We were getting very general reports and some intelligence reports, then Major O'Donnell decided to take his squadron about 600 miles south to Del Monte Air Field for a little recreation, but it was really a maneuver to scatter our airplanes so that they were not so concentrated.

Then, without warning, the Japanese attacked Pearl Harbor.

Our Pacific fleet was literally destroyed and immobilized. The attack on Pearl Harbor, as history has recorded, was a surprise to our government.

My wife and daughter had already left Hawaii; however, my grandmother was still there. She lived on the other side of Diamond Head at Black Point and, believe it or not, was hardly aware of the attack. It was as though they lived in another area, and the news had to come to her by radio.

Panic struck the island. Most of the residents wanted to get out of there, thinking it would be only days until the Japanese would invade the island, and they would become prisoners. It didn't take my grandmother long until she sold her beautiful beach house and took an apartment in town and, a short time after, returned to the United States. The house still remains out at Black Point in Honolulu. Today, I'm sure it's valued at well over a half million dollars.

The same day, December 8 on my side of the date line, the Japanese hit Clark Field full force. And they clobbered our air base with bombs and strafing runs. Many of our beautiful B-17's were destroyed. As a matter of fact, I would estimate that over half of our forces were burned up. We tried to fight back with what we had; however, many crews were without airplanes, and therefore our air force there was very limited in its mobility and effectiveness.

The Philippines in that area became very dangerous because we didn't have air superiority at the time. Most of our fighter planes were very old, and it wasn't long until the Japanese obtained air superiority. They were the masters of the sky in such a very short time. We could hardly put our airplanes down on the ground, knowing full well that somebody up there was waiting to bomb and destroy them.

One time, I was flying in formation with another B-17, and as he went in to land at the air base at Clark Field, he was shot down. Then the report came back, "Don't land here! Go some place else, Godman."

I was almost out of gas, but I had very little choice, and so I continued on to a field called Maravales. It was a rather secluded and unused airfield, and the Japanese did not know about it at that time. I landed there and gassed up. I found an old abandoned gasoline truck, and we read the instructions on how to start it up and how to get gas. Then we sat there and waited until it was completely dark and took off and went back to Mindanao and Del Monte.

For several weeks that became our base of operation, and we flew all of our missions out of there. Quite frankly, for the first several days after the attack on Pearl Harbor, our forces were disordered and confused. It wasn't long, however, until we regrouped, and we started to take hold and began flying against Japanese sea forces—their destroyers and cruisers, transports that were landing the tanks, and Japanese infantry on the west shore of Luzon near Vigan.

One mission I remember vividly was the one where we were flying against the Japanese sea forces that were landing on the island.

As I passed over the shoreline, my copilot and navigator saw Japanese fighter planes taking off. I didn't see them, but what I saw disturbed me more than those fighter planes. Our bombers were missing the Japanese destroyers. Their ships were going very fast, probably around thirty knots, and the way they avoided the bombs was to have officers with high-powered binoculars on the bridge of the destroyers, cruisers, or transports. They looked up at us, and when they saw the bombs fall from the airplane, they would steer hard to starboard (right) or hard to port (left), and our bombs would miss.

The Norden bombsight was very accurate, but it predicted where the ship would be if it kept on the same course. When the bombs were released, the ships would turn, and the bombs would land in the ocean, perhaps a quarter mile away.

As I was flying, I realized that the only way we were ever going to sink any of these destroyers was to get right down on the water and come in at them and drop the bombs directly on the ship. This method of skip bombing was developed later with B-25's. This, of course, took nerves of steel or no brains. I did not drop on that run but turned around and bombed the stationary transport unloading troops on the beach. I made my run in and Sergeant Wallach let the bombs drop and we hit.

Then came the problem of the twenty to thirty Japanese fighter planes that had been spotted taking off the beach. They were now climbing and chasing us. They were right behind us. My copilot sure let me know!

I couldn't see them, but I had that B-17 firewalled, the throttle all the way forward. By now we were around 30,000 feet.

We had the superchargers turned all the way up, and we were going like crazy—as fast as that baby would go. I was probably going over 300 miles an hour, letting down slightly—perhaps 200 or 300 feet a minute—so we could gain extra speed going down. They never caught us.

After outrunning them, we made a right turn and flew over 770 miles back to Mindanao, which was about 4½ hours of flight. We made so many runs like that that I really lost count. It wasn't long until the Japanese ran us out of the Philippines. We then went into Java, and there again were the ever-present Japanese fighter planes.

I was getting a sense of defeat. I felt very discouraged because it was like we were being fed into a meat grinder with no fresh meat coming along. There were no reinforcements on the way. It takes months for a nation to prepare itself for war, and we had not done that. The only thing that we had done to really gear ourselves for World War II was to start producing more B-17's, and we had increased our army somewhat.

Our morale was terrible because our planes were being shot up both on the ground and in the air. People were being killed, and nobody new was coming in. Soon we felt like we were being fed into that meat grinder and the only thing coming out the other end was dead people. We were losing one island, one city, one base, one air strip, one after another.

While we were in Java, we would take off from the muddy field, and all my orders would ever be was to just harass the Japanese. We heard one morning that the Japanese were landing troops in Bali, and here I was with one B-17 and was told to harass the Japanese and bomb them. They were loaded with tanks and artillery for their protection. On top of that, two or three destroyers were in the harbor. And here I came in at 7000 feet; did they start giving my ship trouble with antiaircraft fire.

I didn't realize it at the time, but that altitude was just a perfect range for their three-inch antiaircraft guns. They were going off like crazy under my wing when it dawned on me that I had better get out of there and climb to a higher altitude—and fast.

To make matters worse, there were those ever-present Japanese Zero fighters, and this day I found four of them headed straight for me. One was on each wing and two came in at the back. It wasn't long until the tail gunner shouted up front that he had shot down two of them.

But the gunner who was sitting in the top turret yelled down, "There's one off the tip of the right wing, sir."

And I yelled back, "Well, shoot him down!"

He said, "I can't; the turret is stuck. It won't turn. I can only turn it with the hand crank. I've got the elevation, but I can't turn the turret." But the .50-caliber tracers that he was shooting out of the gun apparently scared off the pilot as we ducked into a cloud bank and returned to our base.

We were so busy that we really didn't have time to fear death. The greatest fear was the unknown. As we waited for the flights, we kept guessing when the base would be bombed and strafed. We were driven crazy by the lack of reinforcements, the lack of new personnel, and the bad news on the radio that island after island was going down in defeat.

It seemed as though the Japanese were a swarm of locusts devouring everything in their path. It looked like almost every airplane we had was either being shot down in the sky or they were burning up on the ground. And we couldn't do anything about it.

Finally the word came that we were to evacuate to Australia. But those first months of December, January, February, and March had been general chaos. What could we do when our air power was being cut to pieces practically every day? And it wasn't long until all but twenty-five percent of our air power had been destroyed.

There was hardly any organization in those first few months because of the lack of communication and the lack of materials to fight with. We were being pressed on every side, but America girded herself and went to work. It wasn't long until she was geared up. And we started coming back.

## DISASTER AND DESTINY

We had lost the Philippines for all intents and purposes. It was in the cards. We had hope, small hope, that reinforcements would come in a short time from America, but they didn't come for six to eight months.

There we were, disorganized and landing in Australia—glad to be out of the war and in a peaceful place with its beer and everything. We were given places to live in Melbourne. What we really would have liked to have done was to get lost and never be found again. We had hardly any regulation uniforms. In fact, I was wearing Australian shorts. We got shoes some place—I don't know how—but we got them. We were, to say the least, a motley outfit. Soon, however, ships came in from the United States with the khaki uniforms, and we began to look like a military organization again.

Being in Australia, away from the war and with many long hours, most of us just sat around the bars drinking beer. Australia had strange bar hours, and during one uneventful day, I was sitting in a hotel waiting for the bar to open, when a military policeman approached me.

He said, "Captain Godman, you're to report immediately to the field (in Melbourne). Round up your crew; they're to report with you."

That was all the instructions that I had been given. It wasn't long until they had found enough of us to crew four beat-up B-17's. I really don't know whether I was picked by choice or was just one of the first captains that they saw. We were told to fly immediately to Darwin, Australia, as soon as the airplanes were made ready. The planes were really in terrible shape. However, the four planes were ready and would take off the following morning. The trip was to take us across the entire continent of Australia to Darwin.

Two of the planes that took off with me, I later found out, were forced to land in the middle of the Australian desert because of engine failure. And one plane was not able to take off at all from Darwin, so I found myself leaving Darwin with a single B-17. I was ordered now to fly to Del Monte in the Philippines on the Island of Mindanao. Rather than having bombs in our bomb bay, we had one bomb bay tank of gas. We were not on a bombing mission, we discovered, but on a rescue mission.

We were also carrying mortars, shells, machine guns, and ammunition of all kinds. I didn't know why they were there; it was not my job to reason why—only to deliver them.

We took off with the intention of landing at Del Monte Air Field at eight or nine o'clock that night. It was going to be about an eight or nine hour flight, over 1,500 miles in distance.

My navigator, Lieutenant Carl Epperson, had given me the course to fly. We were going to Del Monte Air Field where we had previously flown missions against the Japanese. We were told the chances were good that we still had control of the air field there. Later, I found out that the munitions we were taking were to be used by anyone that had remained there for guerrilla action. We really had no forces in Del Monte at the time. But the guerrilla forces were a tremendous and honorable and hard fighting group of men who remained in the Philippines all during the war to harass the Japanese.

It was a beautiful day with cumulus clouds, and certainly none of us had any sense of danger or disaster. I've often wondered if a person stepping into an airplane that was destined to crash had any sense of impending disaster. On this particular flight, I certainly didn't, and if any of my men did, they did not make me aware of it.

Looking out across the sky, I suddenly realized that I didn't have the slightest idea what type of weather we would encounter at Del Monte. We climbed up to about 10,000 feet, set our engines for long-range flight, and enjoyed the beautiful skies. Our visibility was about thirty miles.

It was a perfect day also for us to be intercepted by those seemingly ever-present Japanese fighter planes. In my own estimation it seemed that we in a single B-17 were running the gauntlet because the Japanese had captured the islands on the left, and we didn't know where they were on the right. But we soon passed the island of Timor off to our left and then we threaded through the islands of Buru and Ceram, and I would look down on the ocean and wonder if there were any American submarines down there.

I started wondering, too, what would happen if we lost two engines and had to land. I would look at each island, and I was wondering if I could get the plane down on the beach—and if I did get it down, would anybody ever find us, or would we merely get slaughtered by the Japanese. As I think back now, there was a slight apprehension on that day.

It was a boring flight, and my daydreaming continued with little interruption. I wondered what would happen if. . . . *If* became such a large word. However, my speculations weren't too unusual, for when we were flying airplanes it was a general rule, especially when over land, that we would always have in mind a place "just in case" where we could put the airplane down. These were private thoughts, and I never shared them with our crew.

We were heavily loaded, and our guns were ready for action. We didn't know if the islands were Japanese occupied or not. We still did not have very many intelligence reports. Every once in awhile we would look at the oil pressure gauges, check everything, and check the fuel flows to see that it was on target. Our estimated time of arrival over in Mindanao looked real good.

There is a point en route called "the point of no return." If something happens before that point, you'd have enough gasoline to turn and go back. It was also important to know you could transfer the gasoline from the bomb bay tank into the main gas tanks. It was now time to transfer the fuel from the bomb bay tank to the main wing tanks. We had to do that because if the fuel transfer pumps were burned out and wouldn't transfer fuel from our bomb bay tank to the wing tanks, we would not have enough to get back to Australia.

I told the crew chief to start the transfer of fuel, and I didn't think any more about it. In about five minutes I looked at the main fuel tank gauges, and it appeared that instead of being filled up, they were being emptied.

All of a sudden I knew exactly what had happened. A mistake had been made by the man who transferred the fuel. He had flipped the switch the wrong way! As a result, gasoline was being drained from our main tanks that were half empty. The gasoline was being pumped at a very high rate into the already full bomb bay tanks and was overflowing into the airplane!

My nose confirmed the mistake, and I yelled to the crew chief, "Turn that switch the other way!" By rights, we should have blown up right there, and nobody would ever have known what had happened.

The crew chief then opened the door from the cockpit into the bomb bay, and I saw gasoline cascading in niagara proportions out of the overflow, down the sides of the tanks, and into the bomb bay and out into the atmosphere. I knew then that we were really in trouble. It was a simple mistake. In a moment of carelessness, not thinking, he had flipped the switch the wrong way. We were already at the point of no return, and we had to keep going.

The remaining gas was fed into the wing tanks, but we had lost many precious gallons that had gone into the air. We calculated the amount of fuel we had, and then I set up emergency long-range cruise conditions. We lowered the power on the airplane to get maximum range. It was going to be very close.

I turned to Lieutenant Epperson, my navigator, and said, "Recalculate our ground speed against the gasoline remaining to see what we can do. We are past the point of returning to Australia and maybe past the point of getting anywhere into friendly territory."

After what seemed an eternity in this crisis situation, Epperson said, "It appears, sir, that we have just enough to reach Mindanao if we reduce power and go down to most economical cruise speed so that we can milk the most miles from every gallon of gasoline we have."

Our estimated time en route then jumped from eight or nine hours to ten hours or more. That would put us over the northern shore of Mindanao about 11:30 that night. As the day wore on, we passed many little dots that were islands. I kept reducing power as our weight reduced to maintain a constant air speed as we kept crawling towards the island.

A gnawing feeling of tension built up in me of impending disaster, and my stomach was in knots. Isn't it funny that in a situation like this there was fear; yet, being attacked by fighters, there was no fear of death. The fear comes before the mission, but when you're in the battle, all fear seems to leave.

I really didn't know if we were ever going to make it. I started to descend lower and lower as we approached Mindanao.

It was dark, pitch black. We were going into unknown weather conditions. I had to keep going lower because the clouds kept lowering. Also, I wanted to get as low as possible to avoid any radar detection from Davao on Mindanao where the Japanese had now landed. There was no moon, just an ugly overcast of clouds. The night was just black, black, black.

During the early part of the night, before the sky was overcast, Lieutenant Epperson had taken star shots on three stars and gotten a star fix. After that it was navigation by what we could see. We were familiar with the outlines of Mindanao because we had flown over it before.

Mindanao is quite large, but the outline is very irregular—one of the characteristics of the Philippine Islands. Lieutenant Epperson was guiding me and keeping track of our position by dead reckoning and referring to the map he had in his hand. He told us we were only sixty or seventy miles from Mindanao. The gas gauges were then showing about thirty gallons per engine. That meant we had about an hour at minimum cruise.

That is when we should have panicked, but there was no panic. You can't afford to panic. You've got to remain calm.

Here we were, sitting with the gas gauges practically bouncing off zero. Lieutenant R. T. Carlisle, my copilot, and I looked at each other without even saying a word. There was no need for dialogue.

That ugly black feeling in my stomach was getting bigger and bigger. We were now over Illigan Bay and were looking for Cagayan Bay just one more bay down so we could fix our position. From that position over Cagayan Bay we could turn inland. I thought about the possibility of shooting off flares over the air base. However, I knew they wouldn't have turned the lights on for me, for no code had been set up, and they didn't expect us.

I then turned to the men and said, "Well, there's only one thing to do, and that's to let down gradually over the ocean. We'll go down to about 200 feet, turn our landing lights on, and reset our altimeter by judging how high we actually are. Then we'll climb back up and proceed towards the secret airfield."

I had made a circle over the bay and was circling back towards shore and then paralleling the shore, perhaps about two or three miles out. It was not a steep bank, and if I had hit the water in a bank, one wing would have hit first and the plane would have cartwheeled and exploded into little pieces.

Just as I leveled the airplane out and started a descent, we hit the water at 170 miles an hour with the altimeter reading 1,200 feet!

The plane hit twice. The first impact wasn't too strong because the propellers hit first. I threw both arms around the control wheel and pulled back as hard as I could. The plane apparently went up in the air a little bit. Then it hit the second time, nose down. That was the impact that killed two of my crew members and injured all the rest of us.

We hit so hard that the parachute on Lieutenant Carlisle broke open. I ended up in the controls—my head bashed up against the wheel. I settled back in my seat and by that time the water was up to my waist inside the plane and Lieutenant Epperson had disappeared. He later told me his story:

*I was thrown on impact into the nose of the airplane and knocked unconscious for a moment. My back was severely strained and ribs were broken. I couldn't move.*

*Then I believe I heard the voice of God. I know God was in that airplane. God spoke to me in an audible voice. I had been thrown down in the nose of the plane. I felt this warm liquid, and I thought it was blood from Godman. I finally realized that it was sea water and that we had crashed. I could hardly move.*

*Then a voice spoke to me and said, "Turn left; turn to your left and dive down, and you will come up in the cockpit." I couldn't believe my ears, and then the voice spoke again and said, "Turn to your left and dive down, and you will come up in the cockpit." I turned left somehow and dove down, and I came up in the cockpit by your side of the window.*

Upon impact I thought to myself, "This is a hell of a way to die. . . . Me, an olympic type swimmer who was number ten in the U.S. in his college days, a man who has been raised in Honolulu and could swim all day long—to be dragged down in a stinking B-17 in the middle of the ocean."

Then, all of a sudden, I realized that I wasn't dead, and I still could move. I tried the sliding window on the pilot's side and it opened. I climbed out on the wing. I had on my "Mae West," a life preserver that's inflated by compressed gas. I pulled the cord out and jumped off the wing into the water.

I didn't see anybody, so I climbed back up on the wing. Just then Lieutenant Epperson stuck his head out of the window and said, "Godman, please help me. Get me out of here."

I dragged him out onto the wing and into the water. We turned around and saw the airplane slowly getting perpendicular, and then slowly the tail disappeared.

As the plane disappeared, we could see six heads bobbing in the water, so all of us got together. One of them was Lieutenant Carlisle. Later he told me that he had had a terrible time. He thought he was being dragged down by the airplane because his feet got tangled in the shroud lines of the parachute. He had gotten half way out, and he couldn't go any further. So he had to crawl back into the airplane under water, untangle himself, and then get out.

We found that Epperson was partially paralyzed. It was so dark we could barely see each other. Epperson raised his hand up and said, "My hand hurts." As he raised it up, I could see a dark substance coming out of his hand. His palm was split open.

Then panic struck me, for I knew the terror of sharks. I yelled to Epperson, "For God's sakes, put that hand in your mouth and suck! Keep the blood out of the water, or we'll be eaten alive!" not realizing that I, too, was cut and bleeding. His back was torn to pieces, and everybody else had cuts. So there was blood all over the place. Being raised in the tropics, I knew that sharks hung out on the reefs and in the waters off shore. They followed the scent of blood and the signs and the vibrations of struggle.

I knew then that the situation was hopeless. We would be torn and eaten by the sharks. For the first time in my life I knew I needed Divine help.

For a moment I leaned my head back and looked toward the sky. It all seemed so strange and eerie, but I knew for the first time in my life I was going to pray to an unknown God for help—yes, to a God I didn't know. As a matter of fact, I wasn't even certain that He existed or could be reached.

"God," I began haltingly, "if You get me out of this mess and if You'll get me to the shore line and keep the sharks from us, I'll serve You the rest of my life."

I was saying that prayer for everybody. When I finished, I knew we were going to make it and that God, whom I didn't know, somehow would do something.

I realized we were a good distance from the shore, at least a mile. And if we were going to arrive there, it would take effort.

So I encouraged the men that all would be well and that we should begin swimming towards the island. Epperson could not move, so I grabbed him under the arm and began towing him to the shore. All of us were scared to death. We realized that at any moment the sharks could hit and that our stroking, kicking, and bleeding certainly were not helping.

The plane had crashed almost exactly at midnight on March 13, 1942. I'll never forget that date. Not only were we aware that sharks could be about, but we did not know the position of the Japanese. They could have heard our crash and were coming to murder us. After hours of swimming, panic swept over me again as I looked up and saw strange things that looked like masts of ships coming toward us. However, I soon realized these were little fishing traps which the Filipinos made by putting sticks out of the water to form a V, and in the darkness I'd imagined this was a fleet of Japanese boats coming to get us.

We struggled, and some of the men just kept saying they couldn't go on. Yet I encouraged them, and we encouraged each other. Now, all of a sudden, I realized the shore line was only four hundred or so yards away. My heart beat fast, and I was excited, for I knew we were going to make it. I couldn't help but think, "Just perhaps, perhaps," I thought, "there is a God, and He has helped us get ashore."

And then there we were. We dragged ourselves onto the beach and lay there almost motionless. It had taken us four hours to swim such a short distance.

How sad it was, for the moment I hit that beach, all thoughts of God disappeared once again from my life. It was obvious that we all needed medical attention—some far worse than others. We couldn't stay on this beach; we had to do something, I thought.

Just then I heard a jeep or a motor vehicle in the distance. I gathered the men together, and we discussed whether we should alert the jeep to our presence or just let it go by and remain silent and hidden. We all decided that whether it was Japanese or friends, we needed help. So I stood up, unstrapped my .45 revolver, and stepped out ready to shoot when I realized it was Filipinos in that jeep.

They had heard the crash and had come to patrol the beach and look to see if there were any survivors. They picked us up and took us to a Filipino house. There we were, sick almost unto death, and they tried to feed us old rotten fertilized chicken eggs—

baloots, as they call them.

It was then that I realized that two of my men had died in that crash, and I was heartsick. We were all as one, that close, and now they were gone.

When daylight came, we asked the Filipinos if they could take us to the Del Monte Air Field, and they did. Oh, how wonderful it was to see the American flag and the American men and to know that we were among friends.

The camp was, of course, surprised at our presence, and the camp commander, Major Ray Elsmore, came, and I told him that we had come to pick up many of them. I had just minor injuries, so it wasn't long until I was walking about the field renewing old acquaintances. I found many of my friends who had been stranded there because their planes had been shot up, and they had no way out nor anywhere to go.

Most of them were very anxious to leave because if they didn't have airplanes soon, they would be forced into the infantry or be taken prisoner, and nobody wanted that. We were pilots. We were the fly boys, and, after all, we weren't equipped, nor were we trained, as combat infantry. We could shoot a rifle and a pistol, but we didn't have any training as far as digging foxholes, using bayonets, or taking cover or surviving in the battlefield.

We would be lost if we were forced into the infantry. And if we would be honest, I don't believe many of us would have had the stamina, the conditioning, to do that type of fighting, especially the type that we heard that was going on in Bataan.

Some of my old friends with the Nineteenth Bomb Group and the Fourteenth Bomb Squadron which had been commanded by Major "Rosey" O'Donnell were there.

It was being much talked about at that time that General Douglas MacArthur would soon be arriving on the island. It was then that I knew that the four B-17's which had started out from Australia were scheduled to pick up General MacArthur and his staff. The general was expected the next day.

Now, communications frequencies and codes were being established, and that was needed so desperately. Little did I know that I had been sent there to pick up the general. His arrival, of course, was top secret, but I was determined in my heart that I was going to see and talk with him.

Getting him to Mindanao had been quite a task. He left Corregidor in a PT boat, and they travelled by night, taking shelter in the daytime.

Commander John Bulkeley was the commander of the PT boat flotilla. He later became an Admiral. The PT boats could travel fairly fast in the dark and went almost unnoticed. He had quite a mission, all right, because not only did he have General MacArthur and his wife and son, but he also had his complete staff. On more than one occasion they spotted a Japanese destroyer patrolling the area, and they had to shut off their motors and coast into the shadow of an island and come to a standstill, hoping the destroyer would go by without seeing them.

When MacArthur did arrive, I was determined more than ever to speak with him. After all, I had gotten out of the Philippines once before and now I had been sent up again and had crashed in the sea, killing two of my crew members. I felt responsible for their loss and thought I should at least know what the future held for me.

I went to Major Elsmore and to the Chief of Staff, Major General Richard K. Sutherland, and asked if I could speak to General MacArthur. I told General Sutherland about my situation and the crash, and I told him that I wanted to see General Mac Arthur. Believe it or not, it was set up, and he assured me that he would do everything in his power to see that I could talk to MacArthur and that he would put in a good word for me.

When General MacArthur drove into the camp, he was put into a tent and later into the clubhouse. After several hours, I was ushered in to see him. It was an awesome moment for me to stand before the Commanding General.

I calmly said to him, "General, I was sent here to bring you off the island in a B-17, but we didn't make it. I crashed. Four B-17's started from Melbourne. Two landed in the desert of Alice Springs, and I almost got here, but my plane crashed and my crew was injured, and yes, General, two of my men were killed. I believe that we deserve to get out of here with you some way. We don't deserve to stay here, and I would like to go out with you. I'd like to work for you."

He looked at me and paused for a moment with this long corncob pipe held securely in his hand, and he said, "Godman, anybody as lucky as you who can crash at night into the sea at 170 miles an hour and live to tell about it can work for me."

So, when the B-17's arrived a few nights later, I was assigned to go with General MacArthur in his particular airplane. My crew

46

was not scheduled to go out with me. It was all determined by General Sutherland that my copilot would not go out. Lieutenant Epperson was injured and was put in the hospital far away from the base. He wanted to go. Lieutenant Carlisle was also not scheduled to go.

General Sutherland was frightened that he would overload MacArthur's plane. He didn't know anything about B-17's; we could have taken out many, many more people by crowding them. Sure, they would have been a little uncomfortable; some would have had to stand up for ten hours in the bomb bay, but they could have gotten out.

Lieutenant Carlisle, my copilot, wanted to leave so badly. So about fifteen minutes before we were scheduled to take off, I approached Carlisle and said, "Carlisle, when all the doors are shut, you open it up again and crawl back into the tail gunner position."

He looked at me and said, "Godman, you mean that?"

I said, "Yes. You crawl back into that tail gunner position; that's an order." Now this position in the airplane was not supposed to have anyone in it during take off or landing because it was at the extreme end of the airplane and would be a very dangerous place to be in case of any accident. But when the plane was loaded, Carlisle opened the door very slowly and went back into the tail gunner's position.

After I knew he was securely positioned, I went into the cockpit and spoke to my friend, Lieutenant Frank P. Bostrom, and I said very quietly to him, "Dick Carlisle is in the tail gunner's position. He was refused passage, and I told him to hide back there as he was leaving. So just roll your trim cap forward a little bit because the tail might be just a little bit heavy." We took off without any incident in flight and started our journey back to Darwin, Australia.

It was a thrill to be able to sit up that night and talk with General MacArthur about what was going on around the world, especially the war and what his intentions were with the air force and what our position was, our morale position and our equipment, etc., etc. I also talked with his wife, Jean, and their five-year-old son.

During the night, it was determined that I would be his liaison officer and aide. No thought was given at that time that I would be his personal pilot. I would just be a member of his staff. It would be my responsibility to know about our airplane capabilities or at least what remained of them.

It was just a beautiful night. It seemed to me it was the night of destinies. The Philippines fell behind us into a beautiful, beautiful night. My heart fluttered inside of me, and I was so thankful and happy that I was returning to Australia alive. In the midst of all this happiness, I had no idea what was in store for me in the months that were ahead.

## THE GENERAL'S PLANES

We landed the next morning about ten o'clock at Bachelor Field in Australia. The field had very few, if any, facilities and was surrounded by Australian eucalyptus-type trees, and it was hot! Unless you've been to that part of Australia, you don't know how hot it gets and how the flies stick to you.

After we had all gotten off the airplane, Lieutenant Carlisle disembarked. General Sutherland looked at him and said, "Carlisle, I thought I told you to stay in the Philippines. Why are you here?"

"General, sir," he replied, "I crawled on board, sir, and was in the rear tail gunner's position. I'm here, sir, and I'm not going back."

We stood there tense, wondering what was going to happen next. I didn't say a word; it was up to Carlisle to get himself out of his own jam. If I would have been told to stay, I would have crawled back there myself. The plane could easily have held twenty more people.

The general growled and stomped off, and we all proceeded to the briefing room to hear what General MacArthur's plans were to get to Melbourne. He didn't want anything more to do with airplanes. We learned that he did not like airplanes. He wanted to take a train, but there were no trains from Darwin, only roads and airplanes. So, later in the morning two planes took him and part of his staff to Alice Springs. In the meantime, the Australian government had provided the best train they could provide, and it was waiting there when he landed.

President Manuel L. Quezon of the Philippines was scheduled on another B-17 to carry him south to Melbourne also. When a radio message was picked up, we became gravely concerned that this particular plane was going down somewhere in the desert. Of course, there were no bearings, and they did not know where the plane had landed, or if indeed it had landed or simply crashed. However, when it did not arrive at the next refueling stop, I was asked as an operations officer to organize a search.

I set up several search patterns over the desert where I thought possibly the plane had gone down. Our own B-17's that were available and Australian airplanes began to search. After about thirty-five hours the plane was spotted in a remote area of the Australian desert. A plane landed some mechanics near the distressed airplane and made the necessary repairs, and the plane took off. You can imagine the concern of General MacArthur, especially because of his own dislike for flying, listening to the stories the president of the Philippines was telling about his forced landing in the Australian desert.

It wasn't common knowledge that MacArthur disliked airplanes until after he took the train from Alice Springs to Melbourne. At that particular time, MacArthur had little confidence in airplanes, but later on, as they were used more and more, he had the greatest confidence in them—their safety and their capability to wage war and transport troops.

I arrived in Melbourne, even though I had left a day later, long before the general. I was assigned to quarters in a hotel where the general would be quartered and would set up his base of operations from there.

When the general arrived a few days later, I knew that I had a job to do, finding out what his staff was doing and what work had already been done. It would be my duty to establish good communications and relations with General Lewis H. Brereton who was in command of what remained of the air force of the United States. Brereton was a major general.

I researched to find out how many B-17's were still in operation and the number of fighter planes that were in commission. I had to know for MacArthur what we had and what was their status of operation. He needed to know the instant capabilities of the forces we had remaining. It was an interesting and powerful job because the staff I was working with had no knowledge of the airplanes and what to do.

Here I was now, flying General MacArthur in an old Dutch KLM DC-3 airliner to meet the prime minister of Australia at Canberra, the capital. When we landed, a Rolls Royce was there to meet him and drive him to the capitol. He was only there for a short time and was returned to the airplane for our flight back to Melbourne. The flights going and coming were both uneventful.

Just as I was getting ready to begin my descent into Melbourne, a devilish thought came in my mind, and I thought, "This general doesn't know how tough it is in airplanes. He doesn't know all that it takes to fly one of these things, so I'll just give him a little scare." And I descended at a very fast rate from an altitude of about 8,000 feet.

And as I was letting down, the general got a nosebleed. Someone came to the cockpit and told me about it, and, needless to say, I felt very ashamed of myself. After we had landed, Lieutenant Colonel Charles H. Morehouse, MacArthur's staff doctor, came to me and said, "Godman, you didn't have to do that. When you've got the Commanding General of the Southwest Pacific on board, you ought to maneuver this airplane in a more gentle manner. I didn't appreciate that a bit."

And, to my amazement, if the general realized what I had done, he never said a word about it. What an idiot I was; I could have lost my job over that. Needless to say, I never did that again. As a matter of fact, the next time I got him in the airplane, I made the ride feel like we were floating on a cloud of cotton.

MacArthur was a robust, strong man. He was healthy, but he knew how to rest. He came to work in the morning about ten, and he worked until one. He took a nap in the afternoon and came back to work at four and then perhaps worked until eight or nine at night. This was his usual schedule. The only time you saw him very early was on special occasions.

Later on, when the supplies started coming to Australia, we got a brand new airplane, a C-47. We turned it over to the Australian Air Force, and they refurbished it. They took the insides out and made it very posh with just a few seats. And there was an area where the general could sit by himself with only one other chair by him. Lieutenant Colonel Morehouse usually sat there. If anybody wanted to talk to him after that, they had to get up and stand beside him. It was a shame that the army always tried to isolate MacArthur.

The times were interesting. I was proud to be flying the general, and those back home such as my grandmother and my aunt also were well aware that I was flying General MacArthur. There were cartoons in the Australian press portraying me running around after the general.

Let me tell you, our new airplane was really fixed up. It had pullman bunks and an electric stove and refrigerator, the whole thing. It was a terrific staff airplane for inside Australia. We flew this plane for over six months.

We also received a B-25 that had been in combat, and we "rehabed" it. As time passed, we had to make faster trips for MacArthur's staff. MacArthur never flew in this airplane. It would go almost 300 miles an hour and was also equipped with some machine guns and could put up at least a token resistance if it were needed.

General MacArthur had an outstanding staff. One man I remember well was General Akin. He was the type of man who never sent people—he went himself to set up communications, telegraph, and TWX lines, the teletype lines in New Guinea. I flew him on many, many missions in that plane.

One day I was instructed to get on a transport plane and go to Wright-Patterson Field in "the good ole U.S.A." and pick up a specifically prepared B-17 that would be for MacArthur's use. Later on that evening, before I left, the general called me to his quarters and told me about a B-17 waiting for him at Wright-Patterson Air Base in Dayton, Ohio.

He said, "Godman, I want the plane named *Bataan*, and the artist is to paint a map of the Philippines on the side of the nose and then to have the word *Bataan* printed across it. That's an order."

On my arrival at Wright-Patterson Field six days later, I passed on the general's request to the workmen. They painted a beautiful picture in oils on the right and left side of the nose of that B-17. They were really proud of their work and the fact that they had worked on General MacArthur's airplane. I received the grand tour of what they'd done. The bomb bay tanks and braces had been taken out; in their places were two pullman bunks, an electric stove, and an icebox. The radio compartment had been converted into a sitting room. Furnished beautifully with a desk, chairs, and all, the interior of the airplane was absolutely beautiful.

I was then told to fly the airplane to Bolling Field, Washington, D. C., for General "Hap" Arnold to inspect. He was Chief of the Air Corps. I noticed, however, that to make the rear entrance to the plane larger, they had to cut through the side of the airplane to make the door about twice as large as it ordinarily is. They forgot to put in any braces that would carry the stress around the weakened area. The door was latched shut by two pins.

On the way back to Bolling Field from Wright-Patterson, one pin broke, and the tail started to vibrate, and the fuselage started to twist. My crew chief said, "Major Godman, this airplane isn't safe to fly."

I looked at my crew chief and said, "You're absolutely right, and I'm going to tell the brass those exact words."

We were scheduled to arrive at Bolling Field at a specific time and would be met by General Arnold, who would also inspect the plane. We rolled up in front of the operations building and disembarked and were standing in formation when General Arnold came to me and asked very proudly, "Major Godman, how do you like this airplane?"

I paused for a moment, I looked him square in the eye, and I said, "General, sir, this airplane is unfit to fly."

At that his face lit up like a Christmas tree. He was angry. I mean angry. And he said to me, "Well, I guess there's only one thing for you to do young man, and that's get on an airplane and get your _____ (expletive deleted) back to Australia."

I let the boldness rise in me, and I again spoke and said, "General, sir, I must tell you and show you that I am right. The structure of this airplane has been tampered with, and I want you to let me prove to you what I am saying. I would like to have your permission to fly this aircraft to Seattle to the Boeing Factory and let them inspect it, and if I'm wrong, then I'll do what you say. Is that all right, General?"

He said, "Yes, Godman, that's all right," and he turned on his heel and walked away. Mrs. Arnold brought us a cake which we ate as we flew to Seattle.

I wiped my brow, and everybody around me said, "Major, you really got off that time; we all thought you had had it."

So we flew the B-17 to Seattle with a stop at Hamilton Field just north of San Francisco. The air base has now been deactivated, but at that time it was the place where trans-Pacific flights usually started. We all had our parachutes on because the tail was still vibrating although we kept the speed as low as possible. We tried our best to keep from getting into turbulence on the way.

When we arrived at Hamilton Field, an old-time sergeant I knew, who was the linechief (chief mechanic), walked up to the airplane, took one look at where the fuselage was tin canning and wrinkling, and he said, "Give me your form one," and he put a red cross on the condition of the airplane and said, "Major Godman, this airplane is grounded; you can't fly it."

My spirits rose because here was a master sergeant, a master mechanic, who took one look at the airplane and in just one minute after we had landed had deemed it not safe to fly, let alone a plane for General MacArthur.

I said, "Sergeant, I have orders from General "Hap" Arnold in Washington to fly this airplane to Seattle for inspection."

His reply was, "Sir, if you do, it's at your own risk. I've grounded this airplane."

I countered, "Sergeant, I really appreciate that, but I'm taking off tomorrow for Seattle." At that it became a matter of record that the plane was unsafe for flying. As a matter of fact, it was on the form and became a permanent record.

I flew the airplane to Seattle, and the president of Boeing, Mr. Allen, met us. He had his engineers look over the airplane, and they confirmed what I thought, what my crew chief had said, and what that sergeant had observed. The next morning Mr. Allen picked up the phone and called General Arnold and said, "Major Godman is in my office, and we have looked over this airplane in accordance with your request. It needs structural strengthening in the door. General Arnold, it is not fit to fly. The spars also need to be strengthened. They have stress corrosion. Not only that, General, but two of the engines need to be changed in order for it to be fit for the commander of the Southwest-Pacific area."

By now I was grinning ear to ear. And as they changed engines and fixed and strengthened the structure around that door, I was able to get a flight back down to around Palo Alto to visit my family for three days. I now had been assigned a new crew. Carlisle was stateside, being retrained to return with another outfit.

Now my copilot was a young lieutenant named Walter Seidel from Kansas, and my navigator was Major George M. Markovich, a brilliant man who could speak seven languages.

After my "vacation" I went back to Seattle and then flew the airplane down to Hamilton Field, our point of departure. We waited there one or two days for favorable weather before departing. The plane had special gas tanks in the wings. This was one of the first B-17's that had what they called "Tokyo Tanks" designed for long-distance flying.

I did not want to go back. I hated leaving the United States, and I thought to myself, "If I had the nerve, I'd break a leg." I wished something would happen to me that I'd be incapacitated for five or six months.

I did not want to go back to war! I had had enough. It was so good to be with my wife and Sandra Anne for those few days. However, it made my leaving all the harder. They were both so beautiful. So was the city of San Francisco. Then it was the fashion capital of the United States.

We made the flight back to Australia in thirty-eight hours.

The *Bataan*. General MacArthur's B-17 is parked at Wright Patterson Field in Dayton, Ohio. (Photo by Boeing Aircraft Company)

**Inside the *Bataan*.** I'm in the pilot's seat next to Co-pilot Walter Seidel and Navigator George M. Markovich. (Photo by Boeing Aircraft Company)

**Preparing the *Bataan*.** My enlisted flight crew puts final touches on the *Bataan* at Boeing Field in Seattle, Washington. From left to right are Staff Sergeant Gumm, Staff Sergeant Bone, and Corporal Shoemaker. (Photo by Boeing Aircraft Company)

**My first** *Supreme Commander.* General MacArthur inscribed this picture to me, "To 'Hank' Godman with affectionate regard. Douglas MacArthur."

# THE SUPREME COMMANDER

During the war, promotions started being given quite rapidly. I was made a major soon after I began working for MacArthur.

After I had put on the gold leaves of a major, I was walking down the hall, and the general said to me as he was passing, "Hank, I see that you received your promotion without my help." At that he smiled and walked on.

When MacArthur came out to inspect his new B-17, we could all tell that he was very pleased with it. It was also a relief to me, for the encounter I had had with General Arnold was too close for comfort. At his word he could have sent me to the front lines, or, even worse, back on a slow boat.

I don't know what he said to the president of Boeing, but I knew I was found justified in the eyes of "Hap" Arnold—but not of God. All through this time I had no fear of death and no inkling of where I would go if I was killed. I was concerned mainly about what would happen to my family. I knew I was an American, and America was a Christian nation, and because of that I thought Jesus had me and I had Him.

Flying the general was really safe. It always seemed that when the general wanted to go someplace, the weather cleared ahead of us. We never had fighter escort, either. Contrary to many reports, we flew alone.

One time MacArthur wanted to go to Port Moresby, New Guinea. When the time came for our departure, I said, "General, turn right around and go back to your office because we are not flying today, sir; the weather's too bad."

So he simply said, "O.K., Hank, we'll try it tomorrow."

I said, "Yes, sir."

The next day we did go. That gave me a real sense of pride that at my word the general waited. Our navigational aids in the war zone were really not too good. We navigated by the stars or by dead reckoning following maps. There were certain low frequency beacons that we could tune in on, but they were very unreliable.

About this time during the war a real power struggle developed among the heads of the various services. Included were Admiral Nimitz, Admiral Halsey, the marine commandant, and MacArthur. The issue centered around the question of who would be in command of the Southwest-Pacific area—including Australia, New Guinea, the Philippines, and Japan—and for the strategic planning for the retaking of the Philippines and the ultimate assault on Japan.

As a result, President Roosevelt came to Honolulu, and he called all the "big boys" for a meeting. I flew MacArthur to the meeting and could sense the tenseness in the air. The general was quite confident that he would come out on top.

The meeting lasted several days. The power struggle was dissolved when President Roosevelt said, "MacArthur is going to be 'Supreme Commander of the Southwest-Pacific' area. He will be in charge, and everyone will coordinate their activities with General MacArthur. He's going to determine the strategic plan of how we're going to retake the Philippines and, ultimately, Japan."

The navy and marines didn't like that! General MacArthur gave the overall strategic plan, but he did not interfere with their operations.

However, he did determine the time. He would say, "Now we will take Guadalcanal; this is the time I want you to prepare for this or that." The army, air force, navy, and marines were now coordinated.

One day MacArthur told me I was to accompany General Sutherland to Washington, D.C. We took MacArthur's old scrambled-egg hat back with us because he wanted a new one. *Scrambled-eggs* means gold braid. The general designed his own hat. He was allowed to put as much gold braid on it as he desired. He liked this old hat and the way it was made with the crumpled top, but it had seen its days on Bataan. The old hat was taken back to New York by Captain Kipp Chase while we were in Washington, and a special military hatmaker turned General MacArthur out a hat real fast.

We were in Washington about a week and then went back to Australia. I didn't get a chance even to stop off in Palo Alto to see my family—that was cruel, I thought. I had no idea why I was brought along, perhaps simply to keep General Sutherland company or to keep an eye on the pilots that were flying the airplane.

I flew MacArthur for several more months, and by now he had moved his headquarters from Brisbane, Australia, to Port Moresby on New Guinea. Even though the Japanese were perhaps only sixty miles away on the other side of the island, the mountain range was such that they just could not get across without tramping through the jungle for weeks.

The mountainous terrain in this area was staggering. It seemed as though the mountains were nothing but sheer cliffs. The general wanted American and Australian troops brought in in large numbers from Australia—fast! He approached General George Kenney, and they discussed how they would bring troops, two divisions of Australians, from Australia to Port Moresby. For the first time during the war, troops were to be transported by air. General MacArthur was very concerned that many men could possibly be lost by airplanes being shot down or crashing. This worried him very much.

General Kenney, who was the commander of the Far Eastern air forces, said, "General MacArthur, I do not believe we'll lose any."

And therefore MacArthur said, "Good."

But we could still see the doubt in his mind as to the capability of transporting men by air—at least on such a grand scale. As it turned out, the troops were brought from Australia to New Guinea in record time.

Many of these men went over the mountains by foot along with the Americans and secured a foothold and prepared an airstrip at Buna, and after they had secured the strip and the perimeter, MacArthur decided then that we would bring in the Australian-American troops by air. That was really a feather in his cap. He lost no men in the air although many were lost on the ground after they arrived, fighting and defeating the Japanese and taking the port of Lae, New Guinea.

Troops were to be dropped by parachute behind the Japanese lines in the valley that goes down into the sea. MacArthur wanted to be in on this and to see the operation. Everyone tried to persuade him not to go because of the extreme danger. But we arranged for a fully armed B-17 to be flown by another crew so that the general could see the men landing.

He asked me to fly with him to view this procedure. And there he was, looking out the window, flying in formation with the C-47 troop carriers, and watching as thousands of paratroopers dropped into the valley behind the Japanese lines. There was a lot of fighter cover now, and the troops that were dropped formed up and took Lae, New Guinea.

As soon as they had been dropped, we turned around and went back to Port Moresby. I'll never forget the awesomeness I felt as I saw this general who was in command go right into the dangerous areas of fighting. I personally respected him very much.

(Everywhere I go, I'm asked, "Was General MacArthur a Christian?" Of course he was. He was an Episcopalian and was christened in Little Rock, Arkansas. The general always had a Bible with him—one on his desk and one at his quarters. He was an avid reader of the Bible and a great believer in the power of prayer. The Bible that was with him on Corregidor is now in the General MacArthur Memorial in Norfolk, Virginia. Thank God we had a Christian leader in our theater of operations.)

Shortly after this we reestablished our base of operations from Port Moresby to the northern part of New Guinea at Hollandia. I had my own personal jeep which was going to be sent ahead. The men who were in charge of the motor pool then preparing the vehicles really had taken a liking to me, and they outfitted my jeep with red leather seats. It was one beautiful vehicle to drive.

Before I arrived, General Sutherland's secretary, a very crafty woman, saw my jeep with the red leather seats and claimed it as her very own. She was a WAC. She came to the men and said, "I would like that. I want it for my own." Well, being the private secretary of General Sutherland, she got what she wanted.

When I arrived there, I was looking all over for my jeep, and one afternoon I saw this WAC tearing down the road in my jeep. I followed her, pulled her over, and said, "That's my jeep, and I want it NOW!

And she said, "Oh, no, it isn't. It's mine. I'm General Sutherland's secretary, and I'm keeping it."

I told her to get out of that jeep, and I took it.

Well, two days later I received a call from General Sutherland, and he said to me very bluntly, "You have been transferred from General MacArthur's headquarters, and I'm sending you back to combat."

In my amazement I said, "Why?"

And his answer was, "Well, there's a reason, and I think you know what it is. It concerns a jeep with red leather seat covers."

I had nowhere to turn at the time except to report to General Kenney for duty. My copilot, a man by the name of "Dusty" Rhodes who had been drafted from United Air Lines, was assigned to the headquarters. He had been flying as my copilot with the ultimate objective of him taking my place when I was sent back to the United States after my tour of duty.

General MacArthur was not aware that I'd been transferred and assigned to the Far Eastern Air Force (FEAF). However, when he did find out, I understand that he was hopping mad. But he was such a gentleman that he would not countermand an order by his chief of staff.

When I arrived at my new position, General Kenney said, "Godman, I'm going to assign you to the 90th Bomb Group, a B-24 outfit on Biak Island, to fly combat missions."

"But, General, I've already flown thirty-five missions. I've already done my duty," I exclaimed. "Why on earth are you sending me back to combat?"

He stared back at me and said, "So when you get back to the United States, if you do get back, and they ask the question, 'When did you fly your last combat mission?' you can say, 'Yesterday,' and they'll respect you for it. But if you would say, 'A year and a half ago,' you would be ashamed. And that's the reason I'm sending you back to combat."

Back to combat I went and flew thirteen more missions.

*Bataan* **flight crew.** Standing next to me are Major Markovich, Lieutenant Seidel, Technical Sergeant Bone, Technical Sergeant Gumm, and Sergeant Shoemaker. (Photo by Boeing Aircraft Company)

**The brass.** General Kenney, commander of the Far Eastern Air Force, follows behind General MacArthur while I, a lieutenant colonel, "relax." General MacArthur signed the bottom of this photo.

**Between missions in New Guinea.** War can sometimes be boring and tedious; I'm in my tent—waiting. I was flying with the 90th Bomb Group, the "Jolly Rogers."

## DESPERATE MOMENTS

I reported to Colonel Rogers, who was the commander of the 90th Bomb Group (called the Jolly Rogers), and at the time they were flying missions against the Japanese air fields in the southern Philippines and many of the other islands of Indonesia.

I was very upset and almost bitter about the idea of going into combat again. But I knew that it was the final step before being allowed to return to the United States away from this war zone.

The feelings that would come upon me were so strange. Each of these flights could have been my last flight into some eternity. I didn't know where I'd go, but I still did not have a fear of death. I would constantly think, "Isn't it ironic that I've gone this far, and perhaps this will be the one, and I won't make it."

So many around me were dying, but I had been promised thirteen missions, that old unlucky number thirteen, and I could return to the states. So I counted them: one, two, three. . . . And I marked them off, one by one.

Some of the missions were what we would call milk runs—minor bombing scrapes, dropping bombs uneventfully and returning. Most of the flights lasted twelve, thirteen, or fourteen hours. Slowly I approached the eventful one, number thirteen.

This was going to be a major offensive on the island of Borneo. We were going to destroy a large oil refinery at Balik Papan. Our point of takeoff was Biak Island north of New Guinea. There were to be three groups of B-24's. This would be a large force, especially in those days. There would be nine squadrons, with at least twelve B-24's per squadron. So there were well over 100 planes that would be flying in formation.

In that area of the Pacific there were always tropical fronts, with heavy rain squalls or thunderstorms. Sometimes they were very intense. This particular night, as we began our takeoff around midnight, over 100 airplanes from different bases climbed into the sky at five minute intervals.

Soon after takeoff we approached a front, a huge front. There was no turning back. All systems were "go." The lightning was flashing, and our airplane was bucking and tilting in the turbulence. I was not flying pilot on this particular mission. I was third man, or command pilot, and I had a seat behind the pilot and copilot. It wasn't long even in the midst of this turbulence that I just closed my eyes and went to sleep. The pilot later told me that he was about ready to turn around and go back when he looked around, and "There I saw you, a colonel, experienced, just sitting there asleep, and you didn't even look worried, so I went on."

When we were about 280 miles from our target, we were to begin circling over Dongkala, Celebes, until all of the ships arrived. We would have a gigantic circle of 108 planes, and then we would form in our group formations and attack. We were to have fighter protection which was led by the already famous Lieutenant Richard Bong (Ace Bong). But for some reason they didn't get there on time.

We began the circle. The circle got larger and larger, and we waited for the final group of planes to arrive. Just as we were getting low on fuel to the point of having to go on, the third group showed up. And we were to begin our dash toward the refinery.

We were about fifty miles from our target when we were met by around sixty Jap Zeros and Zekes. The Zekes were much like the German Messerschmitt, and we were under attack for over fifty minutes, all the time heading for our target.

There were supposed to be American submarines off the target in the ocean to pick up any of us who were shot down. I was now standing behind the pilot and copilot, directing machine gun fire from our plane. I looked to the right, I looked to the left, and I was astonished as I saw seven of our planes shot down around me. I saw the tracers going right under our floor with our bomb door open, and I could look back and see the tracers and the anti-aircraft fire.

Then one of the Jap Zeros came right over our tail. I started screaming over the intercom to the top turret gunner to change his guns around in front of us and get that son of a _____ . (It's strange in the midst of pressure how one begins cursing.) He leveled down on him, and as he got right in front of us, he blew him apart, and the smoke and fragments started coming out.

Then I looked to the right, and a Japanese Zero made a head-on pass at a B-24. He dropped a phosperous bomb without about one chance in a billion that the bomb would hit the airplane; it had to be done precisely in a millionth of a second. But, believe it or not, that bomb went right into the cockpit of a B-24 to our right. It exploded in the cockpit, and white smoke poured from the plane. The plane pulled up in a loop, and at the top of the loop I could see men falling out of the side gunner's position, and then it went straight down. I saw no parachutes open.

I saw the wings bend the same way a bow does when you put an arrow into it and draw it back. I was astounded at the structure of our airplanes—that they could be built to bend like that—but all of a sudden they snapped off and plunged into the sea, and the water engulfed it. They were all gone—plane, men, everything.

I stood there in the midst of all this death and agony and flames, and I was so confident, and I felt, "Well, it can't happen to me." It was happening to everyone else, but down deep I really knew that in a split second it could happen. God had His hand on me for sure.

I don't know why, but I had no fear; at any rate, what could I do? Here I was sandwiched in an aluminum can called an airplane, but the consequences of death never entered my mind.

I had had many chances to read the Bible between missions and go to church services that were held even in the jungle. On my air base they had palm leaf chapel, but it had never occurred to me that I needed anything like that. My free time was a chance to sit around and shoot the bull, do anything to pass the boring hours—but not go to church. In hindsight, I can see now that God had His hand on me and was holding me to my promise I had made earlier in those shark-infested waters to serve Him the rest of my life.

We destroyed that oil-gasoline producing facility, and were we excited. However, we had consumed more gas than we had anticipated and could not return to Biak Island and instead landed on an island a lot closer, spending the night there and flying back to our home base the next day.

Several days later General Kenney asked that I be sent to an island where an airplane was ready to take me home. I got on the air transport plane on D-Day for the Leyte invasion on October 19, 1944. That was the day the American troops returned to the Philippines and started their conquest of the Japanese.

It was a wonderful feeling to be on a plane heading home. I had a slight feeling of guilt because of those that were left behind. However, that didn't last very long.

When I arrived back in the states, I found I was somewhat of a hero because of the fame, if you can call it that, of being General Douglas MacArthur's pilot.

The war effort was a big thing, and everyone at this point needed encouragement. So I was "chosen" to speak at different defense plants. They would erect a platform and drape it in red, white, and blue bunting. The employees would be given time off at lunch hour, and I would tell them how important their efforts were in our winning the war.

I did this for several weeks, and then I was transferred to Galveston, Texas, where I was to be re-educated to flying in American skies according to the rules, not just taking off into the wild blue yonder. Really, it was a course of catching up to flying with the new instruments and all the FAA rules.

During this time my marriage continued to deteriorate. Most of the time my wife and daughter were with me now that I was stateside. Her religion of Christian Science was really beginning to bother me. I didn't know exactly what was right, but I certainly knew that the religion she had wasn't it!

Then in September of 1948 I was transferred to Tokyo, Japan, and was again assigned to General MacArthur's headquarters. A few days after I arrived, I called upon him in his office and renewed our friendship. (We were still on a first name basis. He called me "Hank," and I still called him "General, Sir!") I also called upon his wife, Jean, at the American Embassy and renewed acquaintances there. I went to Japan by myself, and about ninety days later my wife and two daughters, Sandra and Gay Louise, joined me.

My wife, it seemed to me, was heavier than ever into Christian Science. She found "others" right away—strange how much I resented her search when I was searching.

Several months went by and then came the test that forced me to make some decisions. Our little Gay Louise came down with a fast-acting viral pneumonia. I said to my wife, "Get her to the doctor and now. Don't you realize how ill she is?"

70

Her reply would always be the same. "She's not sick. She is healed. There is no disease. There is no sin. She is not sick. Henry, don't you hear me? She is not sick. All is infinite mind."

I shouted back, "I'll take her then!"

"Henry," she said, "if you touch that baby, you're responsible for her death!"

Over and over I would hear the same type of logic, and yet I was afraid to do anything. This went on for several hours. That night I heard the baby struggling for breath as her throat was constricting. My wife was on the phone to her Japanese practitioner, a person of great power in the church. She "prayed" on the telephone and said, "There is no suffering. There is no sickness. There is no disease. All is infinite mind." God's healing was entirely up to her speaking and not to Jesus' ministering. To her Jesus was just a good man, a way-shower.

Finally, I couldn't take it anymore. I decided I was responsible for everything that happened anyway. I went into her room, wrapped up my daughter's little blue suffering body, and took her to the American hospital emergency room.

On my way to the hospital I knew this was it! I could not go through this ever again. Our marriage was finished. My wife was silent. She even went with me to the hospital. As soon as we arrived, they rushed Gay Louise into the operating room. They told us she needed a tracheotomy at once. She was suffocating to death.

We were standing just outside the operating room door; the emergency room was rather primitive. We even heard the sounds of the operation. When they put the knife in her throat to let air in, I could hear a tremendous gasp and the sucking in and expelling of air. It was horrible.

It was not more than thirty minutes later that the doctors came out and said that my daughter had died. I stood there in quiet unbelief. Then I turned bitter because I couldn't understand. I didn't understand about Christian Scientists not believing that Jesus Christ was the Son of God. They took Him just as a good man and a prophet.

I remembered later that Mary Baker Eddy had said in one of her books, "The material blood of Jesus Christ is no more efficacious (effective) to cleanse from sin when it was shed upon the accursed tree than when it was flowing in His veins" (*Science and Health*, 1916). Christian Science didn't even believe in the power of Christ to heal my daughter, but at the time I didn't know enough to reject my wife's beliefs.

The conflict was that we could not agree whether to take her to a doctor or take her to some phony practitioner who was worshipping another god. Now our daughter's life had been sacrificed on the altar of what seemed to border on witchcraft.

My wife and I tried to stay together, but the blackness and the horror of that experience indicated to me that if we could not agree on how to preserve life in our own children, then the marriage could not be preserved either. My marriage died right there with the death of my daughter.

We stayed together for about two months and even moved out of the house just to get away from the place and memory where Gay Louise was sick. The body was cremated in Japan and the ashes shipped back to the United States to my parents-in-law near Palo Alto, California, where they were interred. A few weeks later I decided that my wife and other daughter should return to the states. I would go it alone.

I asked my wife, Audrey, to begin the divorce proceedings as soon as she returned to the states, and I assumed that she would. However, she didn't, and the divorce was not finalized for three years.

I really was lonely, and in a moment of desperation I once again cried out to this God I did not know and said, "Please provide me with a wife who is of the same persuasion as I am. God, she needs to be loving, kind, generous, and one who will think of me, be careful of our finances, and try to save money and to establish a home. Please, God, provide me with a beautiful, loving wife. One that I can get along with."

I quit praying and thought to myself, "How very odd." For as far back as I could remember, this was only the second time in my life that I had ever prayed, seeking an answer. I didn't know that God would hear.

## MILITARY PRESTIGE

Shortly after my wife and I separated, the Korean War broke out, and I was promoted to full colonel. I also met a girl by the name of Virginia Russell who was working with the Special Services Division in Japan.

She had been living in Little Rock, Arkansas, with her sister and had wanted to go to Europe to work with the army there because she had heard of all the excitement. But there were no openings, and they told her the only place they had an opening was in Japan.

My first meeting with Virginia was when I called her and asked her if she would like to go to a movie. We had a good time. We could communicate, and she knew the horror I had been through. She was the answer to my prayer! She was a sweet, loving girl. I just could not seem to take my eyes off of Virginia; I was so attracted to the femininity of this Texas native.

It is interesting how at the time I had gone to the Bible and was trying somehow to find the answers. I was still so crushed over my child dying that I could hardly cope with living. I was sick at heart.

Virginia's heart just went out to me, and I soon felt so comfortable being around her and having a person to talk to. She loved me just for myself. I could tell that she was quite impressed with the fact that I personally knew MacArthur. And many times she told me how glamorous it was even to be around me. "After all," she said, "I'm just a girl from a small town, and this is so exciting to me." It wasn't long until I realized that I would end up marrying this girl.

Soon after my divorce was final, Virginia and I were married.

We had a small wedding at Fort Meyers Chapel in Arlington, Virginia. It was very beautiful. By this time I had returned to the states, working at the Pentagon; Virginia also worked there.

About a year after our marriage, I was transferred to Lincoln, Nebraska. Virginia and I were excited about the prospects of having children. I was disappointed when Virginia had a miscarriage. Months went by, and Virginia just was not able to conceive. Then she found a new doctor who gave her medical treatment, enabling her to become pregnant.

Our child's birth was very difficult; however, it seemed as though we both forgot all the difficulties when they placed our little Henry in Virginia's arms. My Auntie Re, the sweet woman I had lived with as a child, came and lovingly cared for Virginia. Sharing these beautiful times brought Virginia and me even closer together.

I was now director of maintenance of the Ninety-third Bomb Group in Strategic Air Command. I continued to move up the military ladder, and I was again promoted and made the base commander. The governor of Nebraska attended my installation ceremony, and Lincoln, Nebraska, treated us like royalty.

Life seemed so good to Virginia and me during this time. Virginia put her heart into being a military wife, and she loved it. I would come home for lunch, and it was a good time for Virginia and me to be very close.

While I was the base commander, our bomb group won the SAC bombing trophy, and our base was designated as the best base in the Strategic Air Command. (What a celebration we had.)

After three years at the base, we received orders that we were going to be reassigned to Spain. Virginia was also happily expecting our second child. We were sent to Washington, D. C., for a six month briefing on customs and manners and also to learn the language. Virginia, who gave birth to our second son, Louis, had her hands full while trying to learn Spanish and the customs of Spain and at the same time be a mother again.

Our arrival in Spain was quite a sensation. It was as though Virginia and I were a king and queen. The commanding general was there to meet us. Lieutenant Colonel Chuck Yeager, who was the first man to break the sound barrier, also honored us with his presence.

To demonstrate the importance and honor of our stay in Spain, I'll let Virginia give a woman's perspective.

As soon as I had found out that we were moving to Spain and was told of all the wonderful parties and entertaining that we would do, I began shopping for some beautiful dresses. Hank really liked for me to be well dressed, and so I tried my best to get the best for the least.

We had been briefed by the State Department as to what to wear. We were told that Spain at that time was very conservative and that I was in no way to wear pants suits or slacks or anything that was suggestive. Manners were everything, and I was instructed to dress simply but elegantly. Because Hank and I were made very much aware that we were representing the United States, I never went out in curlers and always looked my best. They were looking at us, and we knew it.

The first night was one I don't think I'll ever forget. It was the Fourth of July, 1958, and we were to be honored at a great reception given by the Consul General of Spain. The gentlemen were gentlemen—bowing and kissing my hand—I was excited as we arrived; I had been told that there were counts and countesses. Later I found out that most of the royalty of Spain at that time were related to one another, but they were so charming and delightful.

I wore a very simple, yet elegant, black dress. It was very high style, and I felt very classy. The real excitement came when we were to reciprocate with a party. We invited the mayor of Seville and his wife and other Spanish civilian and military dignitaries. I could not believe that it was actually I who was doing the entertaining.

The day after the party I was astounded when the doorbell rang all day and there were bouquets and more bouquets of flowers with cards saying, "Thank you for inviting us." The mayor of Seville, who was a happy little round man with a white mustache just like out of a story book, literally sent us almost a tub of roses.

While in Spain, we had a beautiful apartment that we rented from a count and countess. Part of the payment of our rent every month was a case of Scotch, which to them was far more important than money. At that time Scotch from England was not permitted to be imported. However, we Americans could get it, and so we had quite a thing going.

Carlos, who is now the King of Spain, visited relatives in the apartment building where we lived. One of the things that amazed me so much was the extreme good manners that these people possessed. For example, when a count or countess would leave town, *they would come by our apartment and put a card in the door to let us know that they would be out of town. Good manners and protocol were everything to the people of Seville. We were so careful never to do anything to offend them. It was a happy, joyous time. Hank worked very hard. It was work all day and entertain all night.*

Virginia and I were in Spain exactly three years to the day. Little Henry was now six years old and Louis was three. Most of the time while we were in Spain, they were taken care of by a nurse, and when we got ready to leave, she had become so attached to the boys, especially little Louis, that it was just like tearing her heart out because she had cared for him from the time he was six months old. I was amazed at how fast our children had picked up the Spanish language. Henry picked it up in a matter of a few short weeks and was soon telling us what everyone was saying. He was certainly Virginia's interpreter.

I was now assigned back to Washington, D.C., and became the director of operations for the Air Force Systems Command. It was a good assignment; the Air Force Systems Command had not needed a director of operations because their missions were really research and development, but now they felt that there was a lack in this particular area. Every other command had a director of operations, and so it was up to me to organize their operations division.

I soon found out they didn't have a war plan, which amazed me because if war broke out, they would not have known what to do. My main task was to develop this plan as fast as we could.

As a matter of fact, we finished just a month or two before the "Cuban Missile Crisis" developed. President Kennedy told the Russians to get their missiles out of Cuba, or else! And at that time our missiles in the United States were all poised, ready, and aimed to go into Cuba and Russia. Thank God, the missiles were removed.

After that situation I was again transferred—this time to Holloman Air Force Base in New Mexico. I was sent there as the new base commander. After I arrived there, I found out that a tactical air command fighter unit was to be stationed there, and so my first responsibility was preparing the base to receive them. I went all out because I wanted to receive them in a manner that had never been achieved before, and we accomplished that goal.

I was commander of that base until I retired after twenty-nine years in the armed services, and I found myself thrust into the civilian world for the very first time since I was a young man of twenty-two. Here I was middle-aged, having to discover something new in my life.

**First rodeo in Spain, 1960.** I showed my "western" ways to the Spanish audience at the *Plaza de Toros* in Seville, Spain. Over $3,500 was raised for Spanish orphans' homes and children's hospitals at this benefit rodeo.

**General Gallarza of the Spanish Air Force.** I loved him as a father and told him so.

**Spanish wedding.** Virginia and I attended the wedding for General Gallarza's daughter.

**Bob Hope in Spain.** Military honor has its rewards; Virginia greets Bob Hope as he lands at Morón Air base in Spain in 1959. (Photo by U.S. Air Force)

**Spanish costume.** Virginia and I adopted Spanish ways as representatives of the United States.

**Formal attire.** Virginia and I attended many formal functions.

**Last official visit to the flight line.** This was my last official flight line check at Holloman Air Force Base in New Mexico before I retired after twenty-nine years in the service. (Photo by U.S. Air Force)

# CHANGES

After I had retired from the service, a major insurance company came and asked if I would like to work for them. I tried to explain to them that I wasn't a salesman, but I did have a good entree into the military, and it might make a good job. So I accepted the position as a representative for the Equitable Life Insurance Company—one of the largest in the United States. I tried my very best to sell insurance to people—to the pilots that were going to Viet Nam—but I didn't have too much success.

I remember one man in particular that I tried to get to buy insurance, and he was killed while he was there, and they never did find his body. It was such a trying time, and I just could not force people to buy insurance. I was so very unhappy with my life, and it seemed as though I just could not find myself. I suppose the reason was because I had made that commitment to God while I was in the shark-infested waters after the airplane crash in 1942. Now He was going to hold me to it.

I went into business with a person in Alamogordo, New Mexico, developing Mexican food products. It was a very good idea, and to this day the sauce is still being sold. I wasn't making very much money and was travelling by car and away from home most of the time. And again I wasn't happy. As a matter of fact, I was unhappy with everything I was doing. Nothing seemed to give me satisfaction as it did in the military. I didn't miss the military life, or at least I didn't think I did, because I had made up my mind that I was finished with it, and I never tried to look back. And even to this day I don't.

I went to work again for a company called Dynalectron, a company that was supporting the White Sands Missile Range.

Then I left there and got a job working for General Dynamics in Fort Worth, Texas.

When I accepted the position, Virginia wasn't too happy about it. As a matter of fact, she didn't want to go. It was simply not the thing to do. However, I went ahead of her and asked her to put the house on the market. She did, and then she took it off the market, and she was debating. Finally, she felt she should come, and the house was put on the market, and it sold.

Virginia had a serious bout with allergies. Then it seemed like she went from one thing to another. She couldn't get her breath, had high blood pressure, thyroid problems, even kidney trouble. It became obvious that somebody or something was trying to kill her, but I didn't know who. Everything was against her.

I was a quality control engineer for General Dynamics, and again I wasn't happy. My boss was an alcoholic, and it seemed that he rejected every idea that I had until the company got in trouble and some of my ideas were used. Our lives were in a big mess. And it was to become a greater mess because soon the program came to an end, and the production line slowed down to just one plane a month; 14,000 people were laid-off. Needless to say, all of these people were trying to sell their homes and to get employment. I was laid-off with them.

Other problems began also. Henry was now fourteen years old and had just started high school. His problem all started so innocently—his hair getting a little longer, then his grades dropping from A's to B's and from B's to C's. Soon it went from that to heavily into rock music, and then it seemed that peer pressure was more than Henry could stand. And later we were to find out that he was involved in the drug scene.

We could see his countenance changing and rebellion starting, and then it seemed like it exploded in his character. I told him that I did not want his hair to be long, and I came against him as hard as I could. Here I was, a retired colonel, used to immediate obedience. I'd been used to telling people what to do, and they never questioned it and did it the moment I spoke.

I felt that I was fully justified in coming down on him. After all, I was the father and the head of the house. And it was a shame because Henry was such an excellent swimmer and diver. While we were in Lincoln, he had started swimming, and most of the time when he was in competition, he'd take first place.

When we went to Fort Worth, Henry had met another boy

that had won first place in diving for the city, and so he started diving with him, and it wasn't long until he was coming in second. Henry even went through the "Olympic" school during the summer with the other hopefuls. I was so pleased because I thought this would help him.

After my lay-off we tried to sell our house, but with everyone trying to sell their houses, we just couldn't get an offer on it. I took a mediocre job trying to make ends meet with my retirement pay. Quite frankly, we were just battling for survival, making payments on this large house, and it seemed right now a constant battle with Henry.

Virginia was going to the doctor once or twice a week, and things were going from bad to worse. We also noticed that she was developing a growth in her abdomen area, and it got as hard as a rock. It made her appear as if she was almost seven months pregnant.

At this point in our lives, we were more and more trying to find some sort of a relationship with a god. We had started attending a Baptist church because of the witness of my immediate boss at General Dynamics, Mr. Earl Goodwin, and his invitation for us to come to his church.

It was a good church and had a very good pastor who used to be a star pitcher for the Los Angeles Dodgers. Before long we were attending almost every Sunday morning and even, on occasion, going at night. We were taking the boys with us, and we all seemingly liked the church and especially the pastor's sermons. And I realized then that it certainly is not the building that attracts people but what they are being fed.

After awhile, we decided to join the church because of the pastor. He was so interesting, so dynamic. And one Sunday morning Louis, Virginia, and I went forward to join the church, and Henry stayed behind in his seat. But the next Sunday he also went forward to join the church. And a few Sundays later, all four of us were baptized. It's strange, as I look back on it now, that this experience had no spiritual impact on me.

My life wasn't changed. It was just another formality that I went through, another ocean experience. I really believe one can say, "Yes, I believe in Jesus Christ and I accept Him as my Saviour," in an off-hand manner and not mean a word of it. I believe that's the way I was. It was just words. A person has to fall in love with Jesus before it means something. There was no change at all, and I still did not live for Him or know Him in a personal way. The only difference was that I kept going to church and giving my money. It was a dollar or two dollars and sometimes, if I felt generous, five dollars. Big me, you know—generous me! I'll bet God was not impressed!

In the meantime we were having more difficulties with Henry —more rebellion. He was skipping school. I found marijuana seeds in his window. He had lied to us by telling us it was a biology experiment. I knew a marijuana plant when I saw one. Virginia took one downtown to see if she could find out for sure, and, as I had suspected, it was marijuana. With all this evidence we were now frustrated beyond comprehension, and here we still did not know how to pray.

There was a real crisis all over town with the abuse of drugs, and many of the boys were from the prominent families. And here they were at our house, the long hairs, coming in and out. I tried to love them in my feeble way even if they didn't respond.

But my reaction most of the time was not a spiritual reaction. I would be angry because I was being disobeyed. I did not have command in my own home base. I could not command; the commander could not command! My authority as a parent was ignored, and it frustrated me seeing my Henry go off into the world while I could do nothing about it. One time I hit him in the nose, but it didn't do any good. It just intensified the problems, increased the hatred and resentment, and severed any contact between father and son.

I'll never forget the morning Virginia went into Henry's room to awaken him, and all of a sudden I heard this cry, "Hank! Come here quick."

When I arrived at Henry's bedroom, Virginia pointed to the bed, and it had not been slept in. He wasn't there, and my heart froze. He had slipped out of the window, and he was only fifteen.

Virginia was on strong tranquilizers, trying to keep herself calm. There were times that her heart would beat over 180 times a minute. It was fortunate that Virginia had a doctor at Carswell Air Force Base that took such good care of her.

Oh, how we wanted now to go back to Alamogordo. I thought if we could get back there, things would be easier with the boys, and we could get back to all of our social set that I knew when I was the base commander—all of my drinking buddies. We even considered at that time going to Honolulu, I guess trying to turn the clock back.

Virginia's sickness seemed to be engulfing her. I knew that if she did not find help soon, I would be burying her. She was now scheduled for an operation to remove a tumor from her abdomen at Carswell Air Force Base.

Once, when we were in California, Auntie Re had said to Virginia, "If you and Hank ever get a chance, you should go and hear Katherine Kuhlman. I don't know what she does, but when she does it, people who have come forward fall as if they've been pushed down. Something very strange is going on there. You see people walking up front and saying that they've been healed. I really don't know what it is; it must be some kind of energy or something, but it's really something to see."

One day Virginia was reading the paper, and she exclaimed to me that Katherine Kuhlman was going to be speaking at Southern Methodist University. Virginia started calling all of the churches, but no one seemed to know anything about it. And then one finally said, "I think perhaps Reverend Charles Jones would know something. Why don't you call him?"

Virginia called him and he said, "Yes, Mrs. Godman, there is room for one more person on the bus, and you can have the seat if you want it."

I'll let Virginia explain what happened next.

*Henry took me to the bus, and it wasn't long until I found myself seated, waiting to get to the meeting with Katherine Kuhlman.*

*The pressure of the growth resulted in my having to go to the bathroom many times. When I got to the meeting, I made sure I was near a bathroom.*

*Soon Katherine Kuhlman and a pianist by the name of Dino Kartsonakis came out and began playing the piano. And when Dino played, I knew beyond a shadow of a doubt that the presence of God was in that place. Later, a woman who had been healed of cancer gave her testimony, and I simply could not get over it.*

*I sat there, and Katherine Kuhlman ministered. I soon forgot everything—my illness and all—because I was so inspired as I heard of the power of Jesus Christ. I knew then for the first time that God was alive in my life; I knew the living presence of an Almighty God.*

*I had never seen a miracle before. And that night as I returned home on the bus, I cried all the way. As I looked out the window and saw the moonlit night, I could understand why the apostles had followed Jesus.*

*When I got home, I said, "Hank, you've got to go with me tomorrow. There is something here that our family needs. Please, Hank, call Reverend Jones and see if tomorrow night you and Louis can go, too."*

I agreed that if there was room on the bus, Louis and I would go, too. When I heard of all the miracles, people taking off their braces, people falling down, and Miss Kuhlman calling out one healing after another, I had to see what was going on.

When I got there, I, too, saw people being healed of every manner of disease. I knew that there was a strange phenomenon taking place right before my eyes. And yet, as a man I realized it was all very theatrical. Miss Kuhlman came out in her long flowing dress with spotlights on her, and I reacted negatively, but when she started operating in what I thought was ESP or something, I became very interested in what was happening.

There was a woman sitting close to me, and Katherine Kuhlman pointed her way and said, "Stand up. Receive your healing. If you do it, you're healed right now."

Then she pointed again up toward me in the balcony and said, "People with deteriorated arthritic backs can be healed if they'll just stand up." I looked around me in amazement, and my heart started beating extra fast. This was *my* problem, and I had had it for many years, probably as a result of the crash in the ocean.

I didn't stand up because all around me men and women were standing with their arms upraised, praying out loud, and making strange noises. Certainly, I, a retired U.S. Air Force colonel, was not going to be associated with them. Even with all this pain in my life which I had lived with, my pride was such a strong thing that I would in no way, by the power of hell or heaven, accept a healing.

But that night Virginia was healed. Not only did she receive the physical healing but a spiritual one as well. She had received a "baptism of love," and I noticed that now she had started loving people that she could not love before. She had not told me that she had sensed a healing and that she quit taking her medication.

Several days later Virginia went to the doctor, and he agreed that she didn't need so much medication.

About a week later she came to me and said, "Honey, you see anything different about me?"

And I said, "Virginia, you're not having a hard time breathing at night, are you?" Then I noticed that it was gone! The tumor was gone! I didn't understand it, but I knew something had happened.

My search began. More and more I started reading the Bible to find out what secrets there were in it about God and this man they called Jesus. Virginia had been scheduled for surgery, and now that was cancelled! Everything in her life changed. Everything seemed to be giving her joy, even the colors of the trees and the flowers and the birds. And here I still was with my affliction.

Shortly after the Katherine Kuhlman service, we changed realtors, and the house sold almost immediately for the exact price we wanted. We didn't even lose money when others were losing so much money on the sale of their homes. And for some reason I knew that God had sold our house. Both Virginia and I had seen the power of God in those meetings, and we knew God was going to do something, and so we moved back to Alamogordo, New Mexico.

In the meantime, Henry had run off. We were heartsick and could not find him. Many times he would go for several days, but this time he had been gone for three weeks.

Henry had dropped out of school, and our hearts were absolutely breaking. It seemed to go from bad to worse; we received a knock at the door, and a truancy officer told us that Henry had been picked up. We promised to try to control him and get him back in school, and we did for awhile. And during the time he did attend, it would be one call after another—he was falling asleep in class or skipping classes or being in fights.

Just before Thanksgiving he disappeared again. This was a time when we knew families should be together, and our hearts were being torn apart by our family situation. He came back, and then the heartbreak of heartbreaks happened when he took his clothes and left again on Christmas Eve. How Virginia and I remember that sad little tree. It was such a time of sadness and frustration not knowing what to do or where to get help. It seemed like the only way we could keep him home would be if we were to put handcuffs on him and chain him to the bed.

Everybody in the town knew us and knew Henry as he was growing up. He had taken, as a little boy, the second place in the soap box derby. Everybody liked him. But now he was in another world.

We had bought an old house in Alamogordo, and I thought how nice it would be to have Henry there to paint it and to help us fix it. At various times Henry would come home, and I put him to work painting and paid him. But as soon as he got enough money, away he would go.

Before Easter in 1972 we went to a very early church service. We heard people talking about the baptism of the Holy Spirit, and we needed something because we were so discouraged. Virginia was in the depths of her lows.

Someone had called her two days before Good Friday, giving her advice. The person said to her, "Well, Virginia, maybe you'll see to it now that you don't make the same mistake with your second son, Louis. You babied Henry too much, and that's why he's doing what he's doing." That person might as well have plunged a dagger into Virginia's heart.

Virginia went into the bedroom and got down on her knees and began talking with the Lord. "Lord," she said, "I can't take it anymore. I don't know where our Henry is, but I'm going to lift him up to You. You gave him to me, and now, God, I've given him back to You. Do whatever You want. You take him. He's Your problem. I'm giving him to You, and I'm giving You Louis tonight, and I'm giving Hank to You tonight, and I'm giving myself. I'll give You all of us to do what You want."

She had just read the book, *Beyond Ourselves*, by Catherine Marshall and was telling me how to thank the Lord and praise Him, and the next day she praised the Lord all day long.

The following day Virginia told me how she was awakened at three o'clock in the morning the previous night and that there was a bright golden light shining in our bedroom. She thought it was from outside, and then she looked over, and there was a golden ray in our room and on the curtain, just as though sunlight was coming in. She said she was afraid the light might wake me up. (I wish it had!) She knew that it was the presence of the Lord.

Then I knew that we as a family had fallen into the hands of the living God, and for some strange reason I had peace about it. Henry was still away, and we had no idea where he was. Virginia said to me that we should look for a prayer meeting. I said, "Go ahead."

On Sunday we went to the early church service and were sitting there, expecting something from God. In front of us was a small young man with dark hair. He was in his early twenties.

After going to the early church service, we went down the street to the Assembly of God church and again sat, waiting for God to do something, and to our surprise in came that same young man. Before long we noticed his hands were raised, and he was saying, "Praise the Lord. Praise the Lord." And later we found out that this boy (who was to play such an important part in our lives) was Randy Elliot, a corporal in the U.S. Army.

At the Baptist church we had heard much preaching against people receiving the baptism of the Holy Spirit and that all of this business was from the devil and that the people receiving it were heretics. But I had seen some of these people, and they had something that I wanted. Whatever it was, I knew that I had to have it because that morning at the second service at the Assembly of God church we saw people with their arms lifted to the Lord, praying, praising, praying out loud, praying their own prayers.

I was a little apprehensive for a minute, but then I could see that there was truth there. Here was a body of believers praising God in the name of Jesus. I was so impressed that I went back to that little Assembly church again that night—attending church three times in one day, which was amazing for me!

At the end of the service that night the pastor said, "Let's go down to the altar for a season." I didn't even know what "a season" was, but Virginia and I went down to the altar, and we knelt together.

I just started crying, and I began to pour my heart out to the Lord. I cried, "Forgive me, Lord. Forgive my son. Oh, Jesus, I know You're the Lord Jesus Christ, and I ask you into my heart. Just take over my life completely. Forgive us, Jesus. Bring our son back."

Here I was, the commander of the Strategic Air Command bases and MacArthur's pilot. I had been well known, and I was now in the town of Alamogordo, New Mexico, broken before God, my face buried in the rug at the altar. I had given lip service to the Lord in the Methodist church and the Baptist church, but now I was confessing Jesus with my heart.

I heard the pastor approach, and he asked Virginia, "Does the colonel want the baptism of the Holy Spirit?"

And Virginia, to my amazement, said, "He does."

And then I mumbled, "I do; Virginia's right. Whatever it is, I want it."

So the pastor, and the retired pastor, laid hands on my head, and they said a prayer. I couldn't hear them clearly, and I don't know exactly what they said, but it was obvious that it was to the Lord Jesus Christ—the Baptizer, who baptizes in the Holy Spirit—that I might have His baptism of love.

Then I got up and went home, and the very next morning I had a deep hunger for God's Word. I knew that I had been touched by God, that I was changed and never again would be the same. I turned to Virginia, and I said, "Honey, for the very first time in my life I know, I know, that I have been saved, that I am a Christian, that Jesus Christ is alive and that He is my Saviour. He can minister to me now, and I can minister to Him."

I had now established a point of communication. I felt different; I was different, and I knew it. I picked up my Bible that morning, and I started reading the book of Acts, and then I went back, and I started reading the whole Bible. I couldn't get enough of it. I got a Living Bible, and I read that and marked it up. And then I got a King James Bible and I wore that Bible out.

The entire Bible was just like a color TV in front of me. I saw these people, the men, the women, the children, walking across the scene, and it gave me a living picture. I could see them speaking, and everything that they spoke, I believed. I could see Jesus Christ ministering. I knew it was real—all those promises—my life was different!

In the meantime, Henry was still gone. And one day Virginia came to me and said, "Hank, I need another boy to love. Someone to help me bear the loneliness of Henry's being gone. Could we please invite Randy Elliot to come and stay with us?"

And so Randy came to our house to live. How he was grounded in the Word. He started instructing me, correcting me—what the Bible really said, what it meant. Of course, I had never had much training, but it was still quite a shock to me that this little corporal, this little upstart, would be so powerful in the things of God and talking to me, a retired colonel, the way he did.

But I knew I needed help, so I was willing to learn. And learn I did—even how to pray. As time passed, Randy and I started visiting the hospitals together to pray for the sick.

During this time when God was revealing himself to us, we

became interested in a prayer group that we had heard about. Virginia contacted a man who told her of a prayer group in town where baptists and catholics and methodists and people of all different denominations were attending. Virginia was very interested and decided to go to the Friday night meeting. The prayer group started at seven o'clock, and I expected Virginia home a little after eight; after all, prayer meetings that I knew about were never more than about an hour long.

At nine o'clock Virginia wasn't home. Nine-thirty went by, ten, ten-thirty went by. I had been in bed by now about a half hour, and I got up and got dressed and was about to call the police because I was that worried. I supposed she had been abducted or been in a terrible accident or something because, after all, I rationalized, nobody prays more than fifteen minutes, or an hour at the absolute outside. I just couldn't understand it. But I also wasn't going to let her get by with this.

I wanted to know exactly what happened. I locked all the doors so she couldn't sneak in, and she'd have to ring the bell to make her entrance. Well, about eleven-thirty the doorbell rang, and there stood Virginia. I looked at her in bewilderment and said, "Virginia, where have you been?"

"Why, Hank, you know I've been to a prayer meeting."

And I thought to myself, "That will be the day; nobody goes to a prayer meeting and stays that long."

"Hank, I *have* been at the prayer meeting, and if you'll come next week, you'll see." The next Friday came, and I went, and I saw. I saw the body of Christ sitting on the floor, on steps, and on chairs. They were crowded into that small living room, praying and listening to Bible teaching and then praying the prayers of petition and asking the Lord to save this one or to heal that one or to fill this one by His Holy Spirit. I had never experienced such intensity before God in my whole life.

I started writing down the prayer requests and the things that we prayed about while we attended that prayer group for over a year and a half. When people would testify that their prayers were answered, I jotted that down, and I was overwhelmed to see God answer prayers in such a marvelous way.

I was so hungry for a prayer language from the Holy Spirit. But when people prayed with me about this, I just could not yield to the Spirit. After all, I had position and a lot of pride of self, and I would feel strange. I kept my mouth shut and would not allow the Spirit of God to speak through me. For weeks I read my Bible, and I heard this voice wanting to speak to me, "Henry, there is much to be learned in the Word. There is much to be learned in the Word."

I found that the Lord cannot use a colonel, but He can use a servant—an empty vessel willing to be filled and poured out again. Jesus was breaking me into small pieces so HE could mold me into the shape and character HE could use.

# THE MINISTERING PRODIGAL

In the spring I decided to take Louis and a friend of his on a camping trip to Yellowstone Park. All the way there every chance I got, I kept reading the Bible and books by current Christian writers.

One book, especially, that intrigued me was *Nine O'Clock in the Morning* by Dennis Bennett. In the book he related how he laid hands on people, and they received the baptism of the Holy Spirit and their prayer language immediately. It seemed as though every time I read about this, I would begin to cry, and I'd be ashamed to get out of the cramped camper because I was so red-eyed, even if we were going to town for beans to replenish our rations.

We had a glorious time on the trip. Louis and his friend went backpacking, which gave me the opportunity to stay in the camper and just pray. On our return trip to Alamogordo we stopped at Eagle's Nest Lake in New Mexico to park in a grove of trees. Louis and his friend had taken off in the morning with their backpacks and sleeping bags, so I had the day and night to myself.

I read most of the night, and the words kept coming to me over and over again, "There is much to be learned in the Word." I had been keeping a little notebook and, as I read the Word, started jotting down all the promises that God had given us, the believers.

Early in the morning I had been praying and reading the Bible. All of a sudden this amazing sense of the presence of the fulness of the Spirit of God came upon me, and I realized that there was no way I could hold back now. I was to receive my prayer language at that moment. I piled out of the camper and stood among those tall pine trees. I lifted my hands to heaven, and out of my lips came a fluid and fluent language. I simply stood there in God's vast outdoors and praised Him in another language for over forty minutes.

Nothing was there except the gentle whisper of the trees seemingly saying a benediction over me. No one was there to lay hands on me. It was God, and I realized how gentle and precious the Spirit of God was. I could not help but stand there in awe, looking at the mountains with their snow caps and feeling the crisp air as if all the angels were there singing.

I stood there, not realizing anybody was within a million miles; I looked up, and there stood my son, Louis. He stared at me, and when I saw him, my arms dropped down immediately because I certainly wasn't used to having people hear me pray in the Spirit with my arms raised and walking around in the forest like a crazy man praising the Lord. I thought Louis would think I was crazy, babbling in another language that only God understands. However, he looked at me and gently smiled and said, "Dad, Dad, you got it, didn't you?"

I looked at him and said, "Yes, Louis, I got it."

It felt wonderful, and I knew it was Scriptural that God would see fit to give me the evidence of the baptism of the Holy Spirit. I felt good before, but now I felt wonderful because I knew that I had received that which had been given the apostles and that which the 120 had received on the day of Pentecost and that which the members of my prayer group had also received.

I had satisfied the Lord by being broken and accepting Him as my boss—my million star general, my *Supreme Commander*—to tell me what to do with my life.

That particular trip was about 3,000 miles long, and it seemed as though God had dealt with me every mile. It was such a wonderful feeling to be coming back to Virginia having experienced this wonderful infilling of the Holy Spirit.

We weren't home long until everyone was encouraging us to go to El Paso and attend the Full Gospel Businessmen's Convention. I hardly knew who they were, and someone said, "Well, this is just businessmen getting together who love the Lord and worship Him and want to see others come to the personal knowledge of Him. One of the speakers is going to be a man by the name of Kenneth Copeland."

And I turned to the gentleman who was encouraging me to

go, and I said, "Well, the only person that I know that God is using is Katherine Kuhlman. I've never heard of this Copeland, but I'm willing to take a chance."

So Virginia and I decided that we would indeed see what God had in store for us. We registered, and as soon as my pen had lifted from the paper and I had put it back in my pocket, a couple of men grabbed me and started hugging me and telling me they loved me. At first I was rather perturbed. After all, this wasn't protocol in the military, but I was soon to learn that in the King's army this was the thing to do.

These were brothers in Christ, showing Christ's love for me by greeting me with love and a hug. It did seem rather strange, but I had read it in the Scripture, and after about five minutes there and about five or six hugs, I started hugging back.

All of a sudden I looked up, and I saw this huge, gigantic man about 6'7" with a red beard that seemed to hang almost to his belt. I said deep within myself, "Now, if that guy comes and tries to hug me, I'm going to run out of here screaming."

Sure enough, during the course of the day I passed him, and he grabbed me and hugged me, and it seemed as though my head was absolutely buried in that beard. But when he did it, I didn't mind it at all and was quite excited when he said to me, "I love you, my brother. I never hugged a colonel before."

That night we went to the service and heard a tremendous message on faith. Then the speaker started to operate in the word of knowledge. After about fifteen or twenty minutes of this I stood, waiting and shaking, wondering when he was going to point at me and name the affliction of a deteriorating arthritic back.

The doctors had told me, "Colonel Godman, you'll be in a wheel chair in a few years if this keeps up at the rate it's going."

Then the man pointed in my direction and said that persons in my area would receive the healing of arthritic backs if they'd just receive it. Let me tell you, my hand shot up immediately, and I shouted, "I receive it. I receive it. I receive it. I got it. I got it. I got it." I mean, I didn't wave a claim check, I just turned that claim check in and said, "I receive it."

I was healed immediately. The pain of the dinner meeting, of the three or four hours, disappeared immediately. I went to bed that night and for the very first time in years and years and years was able to turn over in bed without grabbing the headboard and helping myself turn.

The next morning I could put on my socks without pain shooting up through my back, and I knew for sure that I was healed. A miracle of healing through Jesus had taken place in my body. I was elated and full of joy as we walked over to breakfast.

I knew the Lord is alive and had put His healing hand on me, and I accepted it.

Just then this little voice, right behind me, was saying, "You're not healed. It's all emotion, and you're not healed. The pain will come back very shortly. You're mistaken. You're not healed."

I knew that voice, and I turned and said, "Get behind me Satan. I will have none of you. I'm healed, and I'll keep it."

I testified that morning at the Full Gospel Businessmen's Fellowship International Convention in El Paso. We also had gotten in touch with the speaker the night before, and we prayed a prayer of agreement that the Lord would get our son, Henry, wherever he was, back home.

That morning as Virginia and I were sitting together, the speaker pointed at us and said, "Colonel Godman, the Lord spoke to me last night, and your son will return to Alamogordo, and he will also be a witness to the youth of that city." As he spoke those words, we sat there stunned, for I sensed in my spirit that it was indeed the voice of God speaking through him and that our son would return home and would be a witness.

Soon after we returned home from the convention, a man also prophesied to Virginia that Henry would return soon and be used of God in a great way in that city. Being new in the Lord and not understanding the ways in which Jesus Christ works, we expected the moment we opened the door that Henry would be standing there with open arms and smiles, waiting to greet us. But that was not the case, and our hearts seemed to break and we wondered, "Did God really speak? Was that prophecy real?"

But we prayed and held onto the promises of God that our prayers would be answered. And we waited. May went by and then June. And during this time we had called the prayer tower at Oral Roberts, the Katherine Kuhlman Association, and every prayer group that we could think of and requested that they pray for our son, Henry, that he would return and find the Lord. And we continued to wait.

Virginia had a prayer partner who also had a son with a problem. They would get together and pray and cry out to the Lord.

In the meantime, June went by and July, but God is faithful and in His time answers our prayers.

We discovered later that Henry was near Ojai, California, at some hot springs. He had been sitting around there almost naked and had been going to one of the "hippy" places that was so popular in those days. One night an audible voice spoke to him and said, "Henry, Henry, go home; go home. You were happy once at home, and you can be happy there again because things have changed. Go home."

Henry later told us that it nearly scared him to death. (But it really scared him to life.) Immediately he got dressed in the darkness and made his way down to U.S. Highway 101 that runs north and south through California and was picked up and got a ride to the door of our house. God guided and God provided the way for him to come home.

It was August in the early evening; we had just finished dinner when the doorbell rang. I opened the door, and I could have fainted because I saw standing there a tall, blond, long-haired, dirty, filthy son. Tears welled up in my eyes, and I threw my arms around him and held him close to me.

He looked at me as a little puppy would look at me and said, "Dad, Dad, I don't want to be a bum anymore. I don't want to be a bum anymore. I want to be different. I want to stay home."

We could hardly contain ourselves; we were so full of joy. Virginia wept and wept and hugged him and hugged him. Louis was so pleased that his brother, Henry, had returned. By now Randy had led Louis to the Lord, and he also had received the baptism of the Holy Spirit. Randy would come and live with us every weekend from the base, and as a result he was a tremendous influence on our entire family's lives.

Even though Henry was home, we were still wondering when he would take off again. It was obvious that Satan had had control of his life and was going to try to hold onto it and make a last big stand. It was so precious when Louis asked Henry to go on a little camping and backpacking trip, and while they were there, Louis prayed with Henry to receive the Lord Jesus as his personal Saviour and also asked Jesus to baptize him in the Holy Spirit.

Then, to our grief and disappointment, Henry took off again, and we prayed and prayed until he came back. This happened several times, but it seemed as though each time he came home, he would draw somewhat closer to the Lord, and the hunger for the things of God began to grow within him.

We began taking him to various meetings and Bible studies, and mature Christians began praying for his deliverance from drugs and alcohol and spirits of the occult and every other thing that he had gotten himself involved in.

We will always be indebted to Jack Connors and Pastor Bill Buck for the patience that they showed him—the love that they gave him. Many times I saw them on their knees, praying for our son, Henry. It was through these men that he also received his prayer language. It was a slow process, and at times I would be somewhat aggravated with the Lord and impatient because I wanted to see Henry changed overnight, but that wouldn't be the case.

I remember so vividly one night at a prayer meeting as we were praying; Henry sat there and almost went into a stupor, and his eyes rolled back into their sockets as the adversary would come upon him and try to drag him back. But gradually, over a period of two or three months, he was delivered, and he started cleaning himself up and shaping up his hair. There was a desire in him to get nice clothes and to really look like the clean, all-American boy.

Henry started to hunger for the Word of God. He would read the Bible for hours on end, and then he started asking for Bible dictionaries, the Greek lexicon, concordances, and study helps. He listened to tapes, it seemed to us, endlessly. He listened to them until they were almost worn out.

The cheap Bibles that he had first bought were soon falling apart, and I bought him a medium priced Bible. One day he said, "Oh, Dad, get me a good Bible—the kind that preachers use—so that it won't wear out so quickly."

Randy and Henry got together, and they would study the Word and pray together. After about a year and a half of this, Henry started witnessing and speaking to the young people around town. Many nights, long hours after we'd gone to bed, Henry and Randy would stay up and share the Word together.

It wasn't long till Henry started ministering some at the Methodist church with the small children. I really sensed that our son had been ordained of God. He didn't have any papers from a denomination, but I really don't think that he needed any. He knew, in my estimation, more than most people who had gone to seminaries. The Word of God was in his spirit, and he spoke it. He was on fire for the Lord, and he wanted to minister, as he said, just like Hagen and Copeland.

At the same time the Spirit of God was working in my heart, and I started becoming concerned for others and their needs for salvation and for deliverance from sin and sickness. I also started praying for the sick and for those who had bad backs—curvature of the spine—and I began to see miracles, and this brought Henry and me very close together. There were times that we would go out and minister together.

Before long it seemed as though Henry had passed Virginia and me spiritually, and he'd look back and say, "Come on Dad, come on Mom, what's holding you up?"

He wasn't satisfied with his water baptism that he previously had had, and so we went up to a friend's house and used their swimming pool, and Henry and I baptized each other. A short time after that, both Henry and I received ordination papers from a church in Albuquerque. We had been given certificates we could put on the wall; we never used them for anything, but they were there.

One weekend we went to Albuquerque. I preached in a church in the morning, and Henry preached that evening. After he had spoken for about forty minutes in the book of Revelation, he finally said, "That's my introduction."

I turned to Clem Dixon, who was in charge, and I said, "Don't you think we had better cut him off?"

And Clem said, "No, just let him go on." So Henry did, and he taught and preached for over an hour and a half, and God moved. There was a baptismal service after the meeting.

One day at home just before we were to go to Andrews, Texas, to minister, someone walked up to Henry, looked him in the eye, and out of the blue said to him, "Henry, you've got a demon."

"Well," Henry replied, "if you can see that, I'm available right now for deliverance."

That person refused to do anything and walked away. But those ill-chosen words took a terrible toll on Henry's spiritual condition. He came home crying because a tongue had almost killed him, and I remembered in my childhood the little rhyme, "Sticks and stones may break my bones, but words will never hurt me." That came to my mind, and I said to myself, "Sticks and stones can do nothing, but words can kill."

I encouraged Henry that we should just rebuke that and go

right ahead to Andrews, Texas, and minister. It was certainly a hard time there, but love prevailed. As Henry was sitting in front of me while I was giving my testimony, I pointed to him and referred to him as my miracle son, my prodigal son. And then I turned the meeting over to Henry and let him minister. Henry was so gentle that night. The Spirit of God had humbled him so, and people came forward and were slain in the Spirit. We saw signs and miracles that night.

We prayed for one woman, and later she came up to Virginia and me and said, "When your son prayed for me and I fell in the Spirit, I saw Jesus. I saw Him on a hillside and His white hair was flowing, and He was talking to me."

It was such a wonderful experience, and it thrilled us that our Henry was being used of God.

On our return trip from that meeting, we came upon a motorcycle accident; I would say that we arrived only thirty seconds or so after it had happened. We were on a long curve, and it was apparent that they had gone around the curve too fast and skidded off the side into a rock embankment. It was quite obvious that the motorcycle had slid for about 150 feet. And as we approached, we saw the mangled motorcycle and the men's bodies lying beside it motionless.

After I pulled over, Henry jumped out of the car with his Bible in his hands and went over and began praying over the men. Virginia and I quickly joined him as we heard Henry say, "In the name of Jesus, we will not permit shock to set in. Lord, they're going to be all right, and we believe it in accordance with Your Word because we're following, we're ministering through words of power. We confess that they are healed."

About thirty minutes later the ambulance arrived, and the men were taken to Alamogordo. One of the men was a man by the name of Clark Keith who is a member of an Assembly of God church. This accident brought forcefully to Clark's attention the power of prayer and that God's hand is ever on His people. Upon opening his eyes, the first thing he saw was one of God's people (Henry) praying for him. After they took him to the hospital, they could not find one thing wrong with him. He now has one of the most blessed music ministries that you can imagine.

As I think back, that incident is rather amusing because here was Henry standing up on the highway next to these two men with a Bible in one hand and with the other hand in the air praising

God. There were people around, and I can imagine that they were thinking why doesn't someone stuff the injured men in a car and get them to the hospital. But we felt that God would have us wait for the ambulance. We didn't want to move them because of the possible back injury. Yet in our hearts we knew there would be no injury. We knew in our spirit that they had been healed.

There were other times when Henry would get so frustrated, and that would worry us. But there was no stopping Henry. We'd given him a little Datsun sedan. He seemed to have such boldness, and he would go out into the school parking lot and witness to students.

There were times that I was actually concerned about him spending so much time in the Word. He kept saying over and over again, "I'm the righteousness of God," and I certainly thought that he was on an ego trip. The Methodist church in our town had a program that they called Discipline and Discovery. Henry decided that he would attend it. Many people told us afterwards what a blessing he was as he participated in the meetings and how their spirits had been lifted by his knowledge of God's Word.

As Henry travelled around, Virginia and I were both concerned for his safety. But God certainly took care of him. As he would hitchhike, we would find out the various people that had picked him up; one was one of the McDuff brothers, and Henry came back with one of Roger McDuff's tapes. Another time, Tom Lewis, a movie producer, who was a close friend of Katherine Kuhlman, had picked him up and bought him his breakfast.

After another trip Henry went to Virginia and said, "Mom, I've got to tell you about a priest who picked me up. He told me that he was the loneliest man in the world. After riding with him awhile, we picked up a couple of young men, and they were bad-mouthing everything, and I started witnessing to them about Jesus. And they both accepted the Lord, and this encouraged the priest."

It was such an exciting time to have Henry come home so excited with the way God had used him. However, Virginia and I carried a burden within our hearts because we could see that during the almost three years that he had ministered, he was discouraged because he was not accepted. So many people would complain to him because he didn't have a diploma or that he was young and couldn't possibly know so much of the things of God. But we knew he knew the Word and how to minister in the gifts far more than many people that I know.

Through Henry's ministry many young men and women were delivered from the influence of drugs, and it soon became evident that the prophecy that Kenneth Copeland had given was coming to pass. But gradually we could see his ministry decreasing, and he would spend more time praying and working with his hands.

He started going into the hills behind the house with a tent and a gallon of water, and he would tell us, "I'm going there to pray and to seek God." And he would come back, telling us things such as there had been light in his tent.

One day he came back and said that God had spoken to him and said that his ministry was coming to a close. He kept telling us this over and over again. We were shocked and saddened the day he came to us and said, "Mom and Dad, I don't think I'll be here too much longer. I believe my work is finished here."

We had a tendency to just dismiss these statements and felt that he was just into the Word too much and not spending enough time in recreation.

During the time that Henry was ministering for the Lord, I also was receiving many calls to give my testimony at various chapters of Full Gospel Businessmen and other organizations. One day I received a call to go to Las Vegas, New Mexico, to the gathering of the chapter presidents.

Virginia was always insistent that the family would gather and send me off in prayer. This day was no exception. Virginia woke the boys up and told them to hurry up and shower. I can specifically remember her calling Henry and saying, "Henry, honey, your daddy's getting ready to leave pretty soon, so let's all get up and have prayer with him."

I heard his voice call back, "All right. I'll be there in a minute." He went to the shower, came to the kitchen, and we all had breakfast together. The three of us held hands and prayed as usual. As the three of us held hands and prayed, I asked the Father to loose the ministering angels around the house to protect it while I was gone.

I'll let Virginia now tell you exactly what happened that day.

*As was the custom in the house, we always tried to watch the 700 Club. I was also going to a prayer meeting that morning, and before I left, Henry had asked me if I would hem some new blue jeans he had received several days before on his birthday. I washed them again that morning, and they drew up a little bit, but he still* wanted them hemmed more. And I said to him, "Well, Henry, you're so particular. Why don't you do it yourself, and then I'll sew them."

So he pinned them up, and I sewed them. He said to me, "Thanks, mom; you always did sew better than I did." Well, that really wasn't the truth, but I did two pairs, and then Henry said, "Mom, I'll press them." He wanted his crease just perfect so that it would hit the top of his toes. I guess he got that from his particular father and the military custom.

We sat on the sofa and talked, and then I turned to him and said, "Well, honey, I'm going to leave for the prayer meeting."

He looked at me with a big smile and he said, "Mom, you ought to let me go to that prayer meeting. Boy, do those women ever need ministering to." And he said, "They could maybe even learn something from me."

And I said, "Well, Henry, I really don't think there's going to be a meeting, but I want to go over and make sure. I'll be back shortly. I'll get some ice cream, and we can look at the olympics tonight." He gave me a big smile and waved his hand in front of him as I left.

They did have the meeting, and when I returned in the afternoon, the house was so quiet. Louis and his girlfriend came in and had dinner, and I began to wonder why Henry hadn't come home. The hour got later and later, and finally I felt a strange sensation to go to his room. I knocked on the door and said, "Honey, Henry, are you in there?" There was no answer.

Then I felt something must be wrong, and I went and knocked on Louis's door and said, "Louis come here. Henry didn't answer his knock." So we went to the door and opened it, and there he was. He had fallen on the floor with his arms in an upraised position. I touched him, and he was cold. He was dead.

I called our pastor, and he came over in a minute, and it wasn't long until a number of our friends were there comforting and praying with me. No one could understand how I could be so calm, but for some reason the power of God had come upon me and given me peace.

Hank, in the meantime, was in Las Vegas, New Mexico, and I had called there to let them know that Henry was dead.

I had just been sharing the Word when a friend of mine came to me and told me that Henry had died. And he was shocked that my very first expression was, "Praise the Lord." I don't even know why I said that. It certainly wasn't an utterance of my thinking. But I guess my spirit knew that Henry was now with God. I was also praising the Lord that my son, Henry, had found Jesus.

One of the men came to my room almost immediately and told me that at daybreak a friend of his would fly me back in his plane and that I shouldn't attempt to try to drive back at night with the strain that I was under. So I thanked the Lord for that. When I shut the door to my room, I sobbed most of the night, for the grief was almost more than I could bear. The next morning I was flown back home, and I was met at the airport by Virginia and the pastor of the First Assembly of God church, Rev. Wesley Lange.

There was quiet despair mingled with calmness and peace. There was also a strangeness about the whole situation because I couldn't believe that this was happening, and I was very much aware at the calmness that prevailed. I thought, "This is unreal."

It would be wrong to call the funeral a funeral. The service was more like a graduation exercise. Full Gospel Business Men came from hundreds of miles to comfort us. Scriptures were given. People shared. And it was a shame that Henry had to be dead to find out what he had done in his life. Indeed, he had been a prophet without honor.

On the way to the cemetery I turned to the funeral director, and I said the Lord had impressed upon me that I should speak at the graveside. I had thought that I had had something that I should say in the chapel, but there just didn't seem to be a proper time to do it. And so obviously the Lord wanted me to do it at the graveside.

He said, "Certainly; I'll arrange it."

And I said, "Good, because I really feel the Lord wants me to."

This was going to be a little different, for I know that at most funerals they take the family to the graveside, put them in chairs, the pastor says something very quickly, something appropriate is read, and they hurry them away because most families cannot stand the strain. I was quite amazed when almost one hundred people came to the grave site. I never realized that that many people cared for Henry or for Virginia and me.

When I stood up to speak and saw how many people were there, I was amazed. Off in a distance were many ill-dressed youngsters or teenagers, friends that Henry had known and ministered to. They didn't come into the crowd. They were in the distance in the trees, watching.

I said to the people, "This is a time of testing. This is a time of testing of our faith. If you feel sadness and sorrow at this time, then I guess it's time for all of us to re-examine our faith in the Lord Jesus and the promises that He gave us concerning everlasting life. This really is a time of victory. This is a time that a person who dies has gone out of his earthly tent and has gone to be with Jesus."

As I spoke, my heart went out to those young people, for they probably didn't know the truth. Many of them were still thinking that drugs or sex was the answer to their problems. And I wanted to give them love and encouragement instead of discouragement.

And right there some of them came forward, stood over the coffin of my son, and broke down and cried and accepted the Lord as their Saviour. There were even those that later rededicated their lives to Christ.

All of a sudden, instead of anybody walking away, people lifted their hands, and we started singing hymns and songs of praise such as "He is Lord" and "Hallelujah" and "Amazing Grace." I was shocked for a second because this usually isn't done, yet the presence of the Lord came down in spite of what I thought, and there was an atmosphere of worship at the graveside of my son.

The reality of what life with Jesus means penetrated my heart. This wasn't the end. It was the beginning. Virginia and I had been given a new love for young people. We had been given understanding for parents who have lost or runaway children or children on drugs or whatever.

Jesus gave us a beautiful strength and compassion for other parents under similar circumstances. This now gives us the ability to minister and to understand and love other people because we've been there.

It wasn't long after Henry's death that one afternoon Louis came into the room and said to Virginia, "Mom, I was just reading in my Bible last night, and I want you to know that I've asked the Lord to give me a double portion just like He gave Elisha. I want to be able to do what Henry will now not be able to do." So, even here God was going to do a more powerful work in the life of

Henry's brother, Louis.

The Lord strengthens one supernaturally, but a mother never forgets her child. Her desire to hold him close, to caress him, to love him never, never leaves. There have been many a sob and soft crying in the night for a boy who loved Jesus and who has preceded us. There are times when driving down the highway, we will see a boy alongside the road, and for a startling moment we see Henry, and we pray for that boy. A chance remark still brings tears to our eyes, but we still trust and love Jesus. We try to understand.

Jesus comforted Virginia in a very special way. I'll let her tell you how.

*After Henry's death, we went on with our speaking engagements. We had to keep busy, but we felt the prayers going up, and I continued in the Christian Women's Club activities. I kept busy sewing, praying for others, trying to do things for other people, baking bread to give away in order to keep occupied. I carried a Bible with me at all times. I constantly read it. Our comfort was His Word.*

*I searched the Scriptures pertaining to the death of a child and the grief of mothers. It was strange that I never noticed them before. But now I identified with Mary the mother of Christ, Rachel, Hannah, Hagar, and the mother of Sisera; I also noticed David and Abraham. They were not just characters in the book now, but real suffering parents who had experienced similar grief.*

*About a year and a half after Henry died, it seemed that my arms just ached to hold him to me. There was always that empty scooped-out feeling inside. He had gone away from home before, but he always came back. And now I would awaken in the night and hear a car and think, "It's Henry," always forgetting he would not come back. One day I went into his room and knelt on the floor by his bed and cried out to God to help me—to show me something—to give me a peace and help fill this emptiness. Oh, if I could just hold him!*

*That night I went to sleep, and I had a dream or a vision from God. I dreamed that Hank and I were in a bedroom and the door was locked. There also was a chain lock. We were awakened by a knocking. Hank got up, and I said, "Honey, don't open it. We don't know who it might be." He ignored me and opened the door.*

*There were two tall young boys, and they said to me, "Henry is coming. Henry is coming to see you from over there."*

*I looked, and it was a beautiful moonlight night, and I saw a big meadow with trees outlined in the distance, and I saw a boy running with a bag on his back with his arms outstretched.*

*I started running also with arms outstretched. I knew it was Henry with a smile although it was shadowy. We ran fast into each other's arms, and I felt his beautiful, strong arms clinging tightly to me and his warm cheek against mine. I could feel the love pour out from one to the other. It was not just a fleeting moment; it seemed a long time. God was so good.*

*When I awakened, my arms were crossed, embracing myself so tightly, and my cheeks were wet with tears. I wept in my pillow. But this dream was what I needed. It was good; good things come from God. Man lets you down, but God never fails. He is there all the time when we humble ourselves and call on Him. God provided comfort in my loneliness.*

**Our "kids."** Henry, Randy Elliot, and Louis all hold special places in our hearts.

**Mother and son.** Henry seemed to have the Bible with him all the time. He even had to get it in this photo.

**The ministering prodigal.** Christ can use anyone, including colonels and prodigals. Jesus brought our son, Henry, back to us and used him for His glory.

# HEALING

Our son, Louis, is a Federal Aviation Authority (FAA) airplane mechanic, and he just absolutely loves to fly. And our family now has just the three of us, and we have become so close.

When Louis had decided that he wanted to go to college and take an Airplane and Powerplant Mechanic's course at the university in Roswell, New Mexico, we gave him our permission.

The house was so lonely without Louis. We turned a lot of our attention to Lucky, a little dog we had, and it wasn't long after Louis left that the little fellow became sick. He was going to die, and we felt like everything was going to be taken away from us. Virginia and I had each other, and we were very close, but now if the dog was gone, it would leave such an emptiness.

Virginia turned to me and said, "God made that dog; let's put him on the prayer chain." He had developed a large tumor on the back and also some growths on his neck. The veterinarian had told us that Lucky was too old to stand the pressure of any operation.

Virginia laid hands on the dog and said, "Lord, You made the little dog. He's one of Your creatures. Heal him." And in three days every one of those growths around the neck and body was gone. The tumor was still there, and the doctor found that it had been isolated and was able to remove it. The dog is living to this day.

God was working in miraculous ways in our lives, and Satan didn't like it. We had bought an airplane especially for Louis so that he could get his hours in. One day, about a year after we lost Henry, we were having lunch when a man knocked on the door. When I opened the door, there stood a policeman. He said,

"Colonel Godman, do you own an airplane that is registered under the number N8304 Victor?"

I stood there for a moment, wondering why he would ask that, and then, hesitantly, I said, "Yes." Then the spirit of fear came upon me because I didn't know what he was going to say next.

Then he calmly said, "We received a call from the FAA this morning, saying that they have intercepted a distress signal of an airplane giving those numbers. The distress signal was picked up on a frequency of 121.5 megacycles, the emergency frequency, and this was the message, 'I'm going down, I'm going down. This is N8304 Victor. I'm going down. Mayday. Mayday. Mayday. I'm going down in the desert of Arizona.' "

I stood there hardly able to breathe. We knew that Louis was in Roswell and was getting ready for his cross country flight, but he was a good pilot. I turned around to look at Virginia, and there she was with her hands lifted up, saying, "Lord, if You're going to take Louis, too, we don't understand. But we have given both of our sons to You, and if it's Louis You've taken now, we'll still love You. We'll still trust You."

I said, "Virginia, Virginia, that's our airplane." Then I started reasoning that it couldn't be our plane; Louis wouldn't take that plane out without telling us. There had to be a mistake.

I went to the phone and called the university at Roswell, and, thank God, Louis was at school. I called the airport where the plane was kept, and they confirmed that the airplane was there. Needless to say, it took us awhile to get over that. I called the FAA and let them know that we had been the victims of a terribly sick hoax.

It was becoming obvious that Satan was mad at the victories our family was experiencing and the wonderful things that were happening in our meetings. We had seen people exclaim, "I can hear!" or "I can see colors; the gray is gone!" There were exclamations of joy, sometimes almost unbelievable because of the absolute astonishment of the people who came up for prayer.

It is a wonderful thing to see Jesus heal color blindness, an affliction that man can do absolutely nothing about. It is the same with God building new ear drums for people who have been born deaf. These are things that cannot be refuted because they have happened.

People testified how high blood pressure dropped back to

normal in seconds and hernias were healed as Jesus touched them.

One of the main reasons that I started praying for people was because I would look upon them and have such compassion; misery and pain are so rampant in the world today, and so many simply do not know what to do. They've gone from doctor to doctor. They've tried this medicine or that drug or that prescription until all hope has been given up and there is only Jesus left to heal them.

In Albuquerque in June of 1972 I had seen so many people come forward for healing, and I began to realize more than ever before that healing is indeed for today; miracles are for today. And I began praying, "Lord, You're the healer, please use me in this area. There's so much misery and pain. I'm available, Lord. I'm available. Please let me serve in this area."

A few weeks after that I had the opportunity to lay hands on several people with curvature of the spine and backaches, and I saw legs that were of different lengths equalized by Jesus' power.

The first time that I prayed for God to straighten a back, I was amazed. I felt the muscles and the bones adjusting themselves under my hand, and I turned to Virginia and said, "It feels like cats having a fight under a blanket; the movement of flesh and bones under my hand is so much." I knew that I wasn't doing it; I was only a bystander. There was only one person, Jesus Christ, who could do something like that.

Then as our confidence and trust in the Lord grew, we began praying more and more for injuries, sickness, and things of that nature. The very first time I was asked to give my testimony in Odessa, Texas, we were also asked to minister to people and assist the main speaker. Again, all sorts of illness were healed by the Lord Jesus the Healer.

The first time we met Joe Poppel in Phoenix, Arizona, we watched him in many healing sessions. We marveled at this man's looks; you could see Jesus in him. He had such compassion, softness, and sweetness in his ministry.

"Lord," I said, "wouldn't it be nice if I could minister the way Joe Poppel does." We invited Joe Poppel to come to Alamogordo for three days of meetings. He came to our house and ate with us, and we fellowshipped on a personal basis.

I watched him. Deaf ears were opened, and all sorts of healings took place. I thought about this, and then a voice came to me, that small inner voice that sometimes is very, very low and sometimes very compelling. "You can do this, too. I want you to start praying for the deaf."

Soon after that we were invited to Hays, Kansas, to minister. After I spoke, I called the people forward with a little bit of hesitation. "Is anyone deaf, or do you have a partial loss of hearing?" I asked. "Come forward. If you'd like to see what the Lord Jesus has for you, we can pray for you." Much to my amazement people started to be healed; hearing was restored.

There was also a prophecy given forth by a minister there, that tonight we would see miracles that we'd never seen before. I thought to myself, "Oh, Lord, what is he saying." Today it seems that everyone that comes to a meeting to speak is expected to have some kind of ministry. But it was true; we started seeing things that I never dreamed could take place—right there in that meeting.

From Hays we went to Woodward, Oklahoma. Again the Lord impressed upon me to pray for the deaf. We did, and deaf people were healed there, too. We jumped for joy, and I laughed and jumped up and down; I know the Lord doesn't always want us to be solemn. "The joy of the Lord is our strength," the Bible says. I have the tendency to smile a lot.

When we saw these things happening, I prayed, "Lord, You told me to do this,and now that it is happening, with Your help I will keep on doing it with Your blessing the rest of my life."

Needless to say, everyone that I prayed for was not healed. For years many have questioned why and sought answers. *God is the Supreme Commander.* He is sovereign, and nobody can put Him in a box. He's going to heal the people He wants to heal in the manner He wants to heal them. He might heal them from the outside in or from the inside out. His desire is to have them rid themselves of all hate, revengeful thoughts, resentments, and things of that nature. He is going to do it in His time, in His way, when He wants to.

Father Francis McNutt wrote in his book, *The Power to Heal,* that our job is to pray for the sick and leave the results to God. It's not our work; it's God's work.

I asked the Lord in prayer, "Lord, You know we pray for people, and great percentages of them are healed. But some are not, and I want You to reveal to me in Your Word why this is. As I was preparing for a meeting, I was led to read Luke 4:24-27.

Jesus was speaking, saying, "Verily I say unto you, No

prophet is accepted in his own country. But I tell you of a truth, many widows were in Israel in the days of Elijah, when the heaven was shut up three years and six months, when great famine was throughout all the land; But unto none of them was Elijah sent, save unto Sarepta, a city of Sidon, unto a woman that was a widow. And many lepers were in Israel in the time of Elisha the prophet; and none of them was cleansed, saving Naaman the Syrian."

Jesus was talking about unbelief when He said, "Verily I say unto you, No prophet is accepted in his own country." There are those that know Him and don't believe Him. I then began to examine the life of Jesus and how He ministered.

In John 4:34, He said, "My meat is to do the will of him that sent me, and to finish his work." In other words, Christ's mission, His requirement, is to do the will of Him, the Father, that sent Christ to finish "His" work. We know from the Bible that Jesus was always going out early in the morning or at night to pray to His Father to get His orders of what He was going to do that day, week, or whatever time.

In John 5:17, 19-20, Jesus says, "My Father worketh hitherto, and I work. . . . Verily, verily, I say unto you, the Son can do nothing of himself, but what he seeth the Father do: for what things soever he doeth, these also doeth the Son likewise. For the Father loveth the Son, and sheweth him all things that himself doeth: And he will shew him greater works than these, that ye may marvel." Jesus is talking that He himself does only what the Father does.

In John 8:28-29, Jesus continues along the same line. "When ye have lifted up the Son of man, then shall ye know that I am he, and that I do nothing of myself; but as my Father hath taught me, I speak these things. And he that sent me is with me: the Father hath not left me alone; for I do always those things that please him." Even Jesus didn't do things in His ministry until He checked with His Father. These things are true, and the Bible is speaking to us. I've read these verses many times, and when we search for things, the Scriptures light up.

John 12:49-50 records Christ's words, "For I have not spoken of myself; but the Father which sent me, he gave me a commandment, what I should say, and what I should speak. And I know that his commandment is life everlasting; whatsoever I speak therefore, even as the Father said unto me, so I speak." He only

117

spoke that which the Father told Him to speak.

In John 14:10, Jesus speaks again and says, "Believest thou not that I am in the Father, and the Father in me? the words that I speak unto you I speak not of myself: but the Father that dwelleth in me, he doeth the works." I could plainly see that Jesus checked with the Spirit of God the Father before He did anything.

That is the ultimate for us. We should pray and seek God in fellowship, and we should only minister after we have sought Him. He will tell us exactly where to go and to whom to minister just as He told Jesus. And we should listen as much as we pray. We as God's children simply do not pray enough to seek His guidance. There is a tendency to plunge ahead on our own.

Matthew 8:5-13 gives the account of a centurion coming to Jesus. The Spirit of God gave the centurion *the gift of faith* to go to Jesus. And the centurion said, "You, Jesus, speak the word, and my servant shall be healed." The centurion realized that *Christ* had to speak the word; he couldn't himself. And the same thing applies to all of us; not *my* faith, but it is the word of knowledge, the word of God, coming out, being revealed in and through the centurion.

Jesus responded, "Verily I say unto you, I have not found so great faith, no, not in Israel. . . . Go thy way; and as thou hast believed, so be it done unto thee."

A prime example of everyone not being healed was when Jesus was going up into Jerusalem; he separated himself from His company and went to the pool of Bethesda. According to John 5:2-8, He saw a man by the pool who had been sitting there years and years and years. Jesus looked down on him and said, "Wilt thou be made whole?"

The impotent man answered him, "Sir, I have no man, when the water is troubled, to put me into the pool: but while I am coming, another steppeth down before me."

Jesus responded to him, "Rise, take up thy bed, and walk."

The Word says that a "great multitude of impotent folk, of blind, halt, withered" were waiting for the moving of the water. "For an angel went down at a certain season into the pool, and troubled the water: whosoever then first after the troubling of the water stepped in was made whole of whatsoever disease he had." I wondered about that; why didn't Jesus heal them all? He didn't heal them all becasue the Spirit of God the Father said he wanted Him to minister only to that one man.

Several months ago, as Virginia and I were driving to the Phoenix International Full Gospel Business Men's Fellowship meeting in Phoenix, I said, "Lord, I'd like to be used. I don't like to sit in conventions and get fed and fed and fed right up to the top of my ears. I've had enough of that. Lord, please use me. Use me, Lord; I'm available." I reminded Him of this little saying, "It's not capability; it's availability," and, "Lord, I want to be used."

Then this thought came into my mind, "This meeting is a very large and important meeting. Godman, you're too small, no account, to be used in a meeting of this stature."

I said, "Lord, I just heard something, and I want to be used. I won't receive that negative voice."

We had just arrived at Phoenix, and I was in the process of getting our bags out of the car when I noticed my old friend, Bill Pyatt, going into the lobby. He was one of the International Directors of the meeting, and straightway he walked up to me and said, "Hank, how would you like to take charge of the morning prayer and healing session of the convention?"

I stood there motionless and thought to myself, "Me?" And then I quickly gave him a verbal reply, "If you really feel that the Lord really wants me to do this, I'm available. Are you really sure, Bill, that you want me to do this?" I asked again.

His reply was, "The Lord has spoken to me to ask you. Hank, you're the man that the Lord wants to take the seven to eight o'clock prayer session that is so very important to the convention."

With a smile on my face and a song in my heart I said, "I'll do it."

Virginia and I proceeded to our room. I said, "Virginia, can you believe how quickly the Lord has answered that prayer. On the way here I asked the Lord to use me, and look at this. Isn't He wonderful?"

Virginia quietly and sweetly turned to me and said, "Well, honey, the Lord simply heard you."

Every other convention that I'd gone to I went not only to be blessed but also to relax. So most of the time, I must confess, I very rarely got up for the morning prayer session and did not get up till breakfast and then went to the first morning session. But let me tell you, now that I was in charge, I was really excited about that first Thursday morning.

We prayed for the nation and the convention. Yet there was

such a burden on my heart that we pray for personal needs. And I felt so strongly that I should share this particular morning Romans 8:1, "There is therefore now no condemnation to them which are in Christ Jesus."

I emphasized that if you had prayed before for your healing, even two or three or ten times, you shouldn't feel under condemnation because you didn't receive your healing. I really felt a burden that the condemnation for an alleged lack of enough faith should be removed from my Christian brothers and sisters who were seated in front of me. And I cited the two instances in Matthew 15 and Mark 7 where the woman asked Jesus to heal her daughter who was possessed by the devil, and Jesus said, "Let the children first be filled: for it is not meet to take the children's bread, and cast it unto the dogs."

She answered and said, "Yes, Lord: yet the dogs under the table eat of the children's crumbs.

And He said to her, "For this saying go thy way; the devil is gone out of thy daughter."

Another instance from the Bible was where a man had visitors at midnight, and he went and knocked on his neighbor's door for some help, and the neighbor said, "I'm asleep, the door's locked, my children are in bed, go away." But because of the man's persistence he opened the door and gave him what he wanted. There are many scriptural evidences that we should continue praying and not pray just once and simply thank the Lord and begin confessing a healing when we're actually not. To testify to healing before it happens on the basis of our own faith or promise is unwise. That's my personal view.

I've known so many people for years that instead of seeking God have been confessing that they were healed when their bodies were all the while getting sicker and sicker, and they finally had so much self condemnation for their supposed lack of faith that they turned against God!

So this particular morning at the convention a precious woman who had been deaf in her right ear for over ten years said that she had been prayed for so many times but at my admonishment came forward again.

We prayed a simple prayer something like this, "Jesus, when You were on earth, You healed the deaf and maimed; You raised the dead. I believe this morning that You can heal this ear. Praise You, Jesus. Thank You, Jesus. And now we praise You for the results." I took my finger out of her ear, and instantly she could hear. Then the people started coming forward. The condemnation had been lifted.

An International Director who had been sitting in the front row came to me and said, "Colonel Godman, this is the message that we need. Too many people today do not understand the real message of faith."

It's really a sad thing. As Virginia and I travel around the country today, we are going out in the battlefield and picking up the wounded and those who have been wounded by the sword and dagger of condemnation because they were accused of not having enough faith when they weren't healed immediately. It breaks my heart when I see people leaving meetings in wheel chairs, and other people are looking down on them because their faith was not at such a level that they could receive a healing. I wonder who really didn't have enough faith or compassion.

It is interesting that so many of these people that are laying this condemnation on others claim to have such a high level of faith themselves, and I would like to ask them why their faith isn't strong enough to lift a person out of the wheel chair. Did they seek guidance from the Father?

I am speaking only of that which I've actually seen and heard with my own eyes and ears. Some people aren't healed, but isn't it wonderful to know that Jesus loves them just as much as the ones that He has healed.

That morning I was so surprised when a man I knew stood up and said, "You had better listen to Colonel Godman, for just six months previous to this meeting he prayed for my son's color blindness. He prayed for the color blindness of my son and nothing happened then, but as my son was reading in his room in college three months later, the Lord appeared to him in his room and gave him his color vision. He was healed. You see, my friends, the Lord is in charge; we're not. He is going to heal when and whom He wants, the way He wants, and it is for His glory, not for man's."

I was quite amazed and thankful that he would say that because I believe that today there are people running around thinking that it is their faith; they're the healers—look how great I am. I fear for them, for they are robbing God of His glory. There isn't condemnation in a real ministry of God, but it is love and compassion. Jesus had compassion, and He wept.

Today so many people seem to be approaching God as though they had a gun at God's head and said, "I prayed the prayer of FAITH, so You had better act this way." I don't command God to do anything. It is a dangerous thing to put God on the line.

It was interesting how the Lord brought to my mind color blindness and how it plagues so many people around the world. We had been on the PTL Club and were driving back to New Mexico, and we stopped by in Huntsville, Alabama, at a Full Gospel Business Men's regional. Bill Basansky was speaking. I was asked to say a few words and testify.

After I had done that, Bill began speaking, and all of a sudden he stopped and said, "The Lord has told me that I should pray for those with color blindness. How many of you are color blind in the audience?" About ten or fifteen people out of the 600 came up, and some of them received their color vision.

I thought to myself, "Now, Lord, you mean that we can pray for this, too?" That's how we came to pray for Bill Pyatt. He was at the FGBM meeting in Amarillo, and several of us had gone out to lunch. We had gone to a particular steak house on the east side of Amarillo, and coming back, Virginia and I were riding with Bill and his wife, Aloha. When we came to a stoplight, he turned to me and said, "I am so tired of having to memorize the color of these lights—where the green is, where the yellow is, where the red is—because I can't see the color."

Virginia and I almost said the same thing together, "Bill, you don't have to put up with it." I thought that that was a very strange thing for me to say, but I continued, "Have you prayed about it? I believe that the Lord will heal you."

We got to the motel, drove into the parking lot, and I turned to Bill and said, "Let's pray."

And he said, "Yes, Hank, let's pray; pray for me and *I will receive* this healing." In the driver's seat he lifted up his hand, and I reached over from the back seat and put my two fingers over his eyes and said a simple prayer.

I realized then that I didn't have to repeat from memory every scripture that I had accumulated over the years; all that I had to do was speak God's Word. So I simply said, "In the name of Jesus you are healed. Jesus, this is an easy thing for You to give Bill his color vision. Bill, in the name of Jesus be healed."

Virginia also had her hands on top of his head, and in her

very sweet voice and just like a woman she said, "Lord, let him see the colors of the rainbow."

Bill opened his eyes and started seeing colors! And that night he gave a testimony in front of 2000 people. He started pointing out the color of the women's dresses in the audience. And then a man in the audience that was color blind had his eyes start to water, and Jesus touched him as Bill was giving his testimony, and without even a prayer being offered, Jesus gave him his color vision. No man could take credit or even dare take credit for that healing. It was simply the *Word* going forth.

God wants us to go forth and bear fruit in His name. The Lord had spoken to me many months prior, "Remember that when you touch someone that it is Me touching them. When you embrace someone that it is Me embracing them. When you love someone, it is Me loving them. And, Hank, always remember that, and you will always walk in the truth of My Word."

You see, as we walk in His footsteps, we are speaking His Word. And He has promised that His Word will go forth and accomplish that which He pleases. So there's the difference between babbling, mouthing, or just our religious theories. We must speak forth the Word of God, and then we have the assurance that God will work.

In the Spring of 1979 I was invited to be a principal speaker at the Full Gospel Business Men's Regional Convention in Dogpatch, Arkansas. It was not by accident that I was there. The arrangement had been made in a very complicated way by meeting a certain man from Arkansas in El Paso, Texas, and striking up a conversation and so forth and so on.

I was scheduled to be the Friday night speaker. After having the morning prayer and healing session and listening to the teaching sessions, I went to my room after lunch and tried to rest, for I knew that the evening session would be long and hard. I would need my composure, and I would need to relax and completely clear my mind so that I could speak what God wanted me to speak.

As I lay down on the bed to nap, God started to speak to me in words and signs and flashes of light in arrows. And the arrows would go across the vision in my mind with the word, "Repent. Tell the people to repent. Tell them that they have taken the gifts that I have given to the body of Christ and they have run with them. They have taken them without repentance. Tell them that the kingdom of God has already come to them, but now it is coming even closer."

I tried to get rest; I tried to dismiss it, but these arrows in the shape of *repent* kept coming across in all sorts of different angles, and I was disturbed. I thought to myself, "Is this You, Lord?" Then I realized that it had to be. Who else would want His body of believers to repent?

That night when the time came for me to speak, and I had spoken for about thirty minutes, there was a pause while the person that was taping my message came to the end of the tape, and the voice came to me and the Lord said, "Now, Hank, tell them now."

So I backed away from the microphone and lifted up my head, and I stretched out my arms toward the crowd and then lifted them up to God, and I spoke with the loudest voice that I as a colonel had ever used. And I said, "Repent! repent! repent! You have taken My gifts and run with them without repentance. Repent, repent."

I then continued with my testimony for about another twenty minutes; then I ministered. I noticed a strange thing that as they dismissed in prayer, everyone was standing, and no one seemed to want to move. As I walked down onto the main floor, about thirty people came forward for ministering. I stood there for about an hour and a half and hardly a person left. And finally they started to sit down, and people still came forward.

I don't remember what healings took place or what happened. There were many that came forward for the infilling of the Holy Spirit. I never keep a record because I realize that it is the Lord's work and not mine.

The next morning many people came to me and said that they had gone home and gotten on their knees and repented for most of the night. They prayed repentance for the first time in their lives. Many came and said to Virginia that as I spoke that night and gave that prophecy, I was outlined with light.

I feel very strongly that the message of repentance is for all today. The Scripture tells us that there is no salvation without repentance. The Lord wants us to make a 180 degree turn, as we say in aviation circles, a complete turnabout from our present way of life to the life that He wants us to have in Jesus. He wants us to walk from darkness to light. There is no gray area with the Lord. John the Baptist preached it. Why did he preach that?

Because he knew that in Jesus there must be repentance.

Today I give this message many times. Not as a fresh prophecy—I would never attempt to fool anybody—but as a prophecy that God had given me at Dogpatch, because the message of repentance is for the whole world today because Jesus is coming, and He is coming soon.

Charles Price in his book, *The Real Faith*, published by Logos, stated this: "We must face facts. It is not pleasing to the Holy Spirit to dismiss the evident discrepancy between theology and experiences with a shrug of the shoulders and refuse to ask for light and guidance in all important problems. Only the truth can make us free from the bondage of fear and doubt and discouragement that ultimately comes at the end of the road of disappointments. The only way to get the truth is to come in sincerity and absolute honesty of heart and mind to Jesus our Lord."

Our Lord said that He himself is the truth, and as we open the door of our heart to Him, He makes possible the complete revelation that only His presence can bring. Even so, come Lord Jesus!